AF560686

INDIA IN THE MIRROR OF FOREIGN DIPLOMATIC ARCHIVES

Centre de Sciences Humaines (Centre for Social Sciences and Humanities): Created in New Delhi in 1989 the CSH, is part of network of reserach centres of the French Ministry of Foreign Affairs. The Centre's research work is primarily oriented towards the study of issues concerning the contemporary dynamics of development in India and South Asia. The activities of the Centre are focused on four main themes, namely: Economic growth and sustainable development, International and regional relations, Institutional structures and political constructions of identity and Urban dynamics.

(Centre de Sciences Humaines, 2, Aurangzeb Road, New Delhi 110011, India, Tel: (91 11) 23 01 62 59/23 01 41 73, Fax: (91 11) 23 01 84 80, E-mail: public@csh-delhi.com, Website: http://www.csh-delhi.com)

Institut Français de Pondichéry (French Institute of Pondicherry): Created in 1955, the IFP is a multidisciplinary research and advanced educational institute. Major research works are focusing on Sanskrit and Tamil Languages and literatures—in close collaboration with the *Ecole Française d'Extrême-Orient*—ecosystems, biodiversity and sustainability, dynamics of population and socio-economic development.

(Institut Français de Pondichéry, 11, Saint Louis Street, P.B. 33 Pondicherry 605 001, Tel: (91 413) 23 34 170/23 34 168, Telex: 469224 FRAN-In, Fax: (91 413) 23 39 534, E-mail: ifpdir@ifpindia.org, Website: http://www.ifpindia.org.)

India in the Mirror of Foreign Diplomatic Archieves

Edited by

MAX-JEAN ZINS

GILLES BOQUÉRAT

MANOHAR

CENTRE DE SCIENCES HUMAINES

2004

First published 2004

ISBN 81-7304-535-6

Published by
Ajay Kumar Jain for
Manohar Publishers & Distributors
4753/23 Ansari Road, Daryaganj
New Delhi 110 002

Typeset by
Ajay Art, Delhi 110 085

Printed at
Lordson Publishers Pvt. Ltd.
Delhi 110 007

Contents

❖ Introduction

Since India's independence, the output of literature on its foreign policy has been prodigious. This country of more than one billion inhabitants is one of the most significant powers in the world today and its geopolitical stature will probably increase in the coming decades, as will the foreign relations literature. However, until now none of the existing literature is based on Indian archival documents for the simple reason that significant diplomatic records are kept locked and not even through restricted-circulation could the political scientists and historians have access to them. There is a veil of secrecy in India that other major democratic countries lifted long ago. Even countries which did not fall in this category until recently, have shown greater openness. For instance, after the fall of the Berlin Wall, Russia started opening its governmental and Communist Party archives to a significant extent.

The United States Government archives are the most easily accessible records, due to the numerous volumes of the *Foreign Relations of the United States* (FRUS) series produced by the State Department's Office of the Historian. The latest volume published for South Asia covers the Lyndon Johnson administration (1964-8). The FRUS series contain documents from presidential libraries, Departments of State and Defence, National Security Council, Central Intelligence Agency, Agency for International Development and other foreign affairs agencies as well as private papers of individuals involved in formulating US foreign policy and transcripts prepared from presidential tape-recordings. After his departure from office, each American president is legally bound to deposit in the archives, historical materials created and received by the White House. Documentation related to the Nixon administration (1969-74), which is of fundamental interest to understand the US policy towards India and China in the early 1970s, has been recently opened to the public. The Public Record Office in London permits an easy access to the Foreign Office and the Commonwealth Relations Office's archives for the post-Independence era. As it strictly follows the thirty years rule prescription, the British perception and attitude vis-à-vis India can be studied until the Bangladesh crisis of

1971. The same rule applies to the diplomatic archives of the French Ministry of Foreign Affairs. Though these countries do not allow the public to consult every document; according to its own national legislation, each administration maintains the right not to communicate the documents it considers too sensitive and therefore submits it to a longer prescription period. Nevertheless, one can say that the bulk of the documents, in fact the most essential part, can be freely consulted and analysed. India unfortunately does not follow this tradition and practice. This does not mean that we are totally ignorant of the India's foreign policy-making process, thanks to the remarkable series of *Selected Works of Jawaharlal Nehru*. This extensive compilation of first-hand documents was until recently edited by the late Sarvepalli Gopal who had also written a well-known biograghy of the first Prime Minister of India enriched by a privileged access to Nehru's private papers. However, besides the fact that it may take another decade before the whole Nehru era is covered, it remains an incomplete picture of the official historical record on external relations and diplomatic activity.

The idea of this book proceeds from the co-existence of Indian secrecy that stifles academic inquiry and the release of significant materials from foreign archives which offers the fascinating possibility of understanding India's external policy through the primary sources of others. One should recognize indeed that such a detour does not *per se* solve the problem totally. The foreign archives of the United States, the former Soviet Union, the United Kingdom or France cannot be taken as a direct reflection of India's external policy. They certainly can play the role of a mirror, but even the most perfect mirror will give only an unidimensional image of the reality. For instance, whenever a foreign diplomat reports a conversation he has had with an Indian counterpart, his words cannot be necessarily construed as the exact reflection of the message that his Indian colleague's words wanted to convey. It has to be seen through the prism of his understanding of India, national interest or what is perceived as such, notion of priorities, position in the policy-making process at home, or the use of language in the broader sense. In other words, his own bias will always constitute a screen between his own reality and India's reality. The same can also be said regarding any analyses on foreign policy decisions. The diplomat's glance is nevertheless of great value. After all, American, British, French or Soviet diplomatic testimony can be presumed a reliable, reasonable record of events and a competent attempt to inform their administration as objectively as possible, without distortion—at least consciously—about what the Indians have to tell them. Furthermore, the comparison of different national approach is an incomparable tool to define the multiple dimensions of a problem. The detour via the foreign diplomatic archives can help us overcome to some extent, the non-access to the Indian records and gives us a better comprehension of what drove bilateral relations. At least this is the objective of this book, which represents the first attempt in this direction.

The historical period covered by the archives is also of special interest on two accounts. It was firstly the elaboration of India's foreign policy immediately after Independence in 1947. India had to evolve its external policy in a sharply polarized world and the international community was curious about it. Big issues were at stake and India's first moves were watched with interest and attention. The British were, no doubt, the best connoisseurs of India at that time. Their contacts with India were numerous and deep and they were able to save many of their interests through the peaceful transfer of power. Their interviews with Indian diplomats reveals this closeness. By contrast, the Soviet diplomatic contacts with the Indian political and administrative elite was extremely tenuous and rather distrustful and the level of relations developed significantly only after Stalin's death in March 1953. With regard to France, who still had some possessions in India, the approach vis-à-vis New Delhi was largely blurred by the upheavals in its colonies that found a sympathetic echo in the anti-imperialist agenda of the Indian leadership. The American administration in 1947, was well aware of the basic problems of India's foreign policy even if they still acted partly on the advice of their British allies. They soon developed a policy of their own, supported by an unequalled capacity to assist India's economic development, more so from the mid-1950s onwards, especially after the disastrous Suez crisis which dealt a blow to the British influence in South Asia.

The period for which the archival documents have been consulted is, secondly, significant because it deals with a large part of the Cold War era. The long succession of letters, notes and reports sent by the American, British, French and Soviet diplomats posted in India represents more than a daily chronicle of three decades of international politics. It helps to understand the structure of a changing world and the way India tried to find its way in this environment and pursue its national interest. In this regard, the American archives, notably the Nixon's papers, help us clarify some aspects of New Delhi's external policy vis-à-vis China. Everything happens as if the Cold War era could be divided in two main sub-periods, before and after the Sino-Soviet split of the early 1960s to which India contributed significantly. Once the Nixon administration understands the benefits it can draw from the division of the Communist bloc, India finds itself in a new situation, having to face two inimical powers—the USA and China—which have decided to forge a 'tacit alliance', to quote Henry Kissinger, against the Soviet Union. Winston Lord, a close adviser of Kissinger and the head of the American Policy Planning Staff, did suggest tongue-in-cheek to the Chinese leaders that it would be nice to give nuclear weapons to Pakistan and Bangladesh to counter India's hegemony in South Asia. This was of course a joke, but such cynical proposition illustrates nevertheless, the new atmosphere prevailing in the 1970s between the USA and China, in sharp contrast with the one of the 1960s and 1950s. In this regard, the content of the discussions between Indian diplomats and their American colleagues, as reported by the latter, can help us to understand better how the Indian diplomacy decided to react to this evolving world configuration.

The reader may be surprised sometimes to discover the words used by the Indian diplomats to defend or to expose the policy of their government. One may even doubt their veracity. The fact, however, is that they are duly reported in the archives of the concerned countries. One can also hope that the day when it will be possible to cross-check what is being highlighted in this book with India's public records is not too far ahead. The papers published here are based on contributions made during an international seminar held in New Delhi on 14-15 March 2002 under the auspices of the Centre de Sciences Humaines, New Delhi, the CERI (Centre d'Etudes et de Recherches Internationales), Paris, and the India International Centre, New Delhi. We would like to thank the distinguished academics and former ambassadors who contributed in various ways to the success of this seminar.

October 2003

MAX-JEAN ZINS
GILLES BOQUÉRAT

GILLES BOQUÉRAT

France's Political Interaction with India through the Quai d'Orsay Archives (1947-1972)

Unlike the active involvement of the United States or the United Kingdom in engaging New Delhi to further their geo-strategic interests or in promoting a democratic India as a counter-model to Communist China, there was nothing like a clearly defined French policy vis-à-vis India which would be part and parcel of a larger Asian or global vision. The British, for instance, considered that, 'the importance of denying India to the Communist side is almost as great as that of preventing France from sliding behind the iron curtain in the post-war years'.[1] Nothing like, on the other side, the Soviet determination to find favour with the Indian leaders so as to use India as a springboard to counter American and Chinese influences in Asia. France remained largely an observer of India's involvement in regional and world affairs and became only an actor, direct or indirect, on the colonial question which cast a shadow over the bilateral relations till the early 1960s. It was difficult for France to comprehend India as a modern political entity of significant interest. The fascination for India had more to do with its past. This was reflected for instance in the words of Rajeshwar Dayal, the Indian Ambassador to France in 1965-6: 'Never was a country more conscious of India's ancient culture and civilisation than France. . . . The high dignitaries on whom I called would almost invariably refer to India's ancient heritage, and even so prosaic a functionary as the Governor of the Bank of France could talk of little else.[2] Semantically, it is also worth noticing that Count Ostrorog, the longest serving French Ambassador to India (June 1951-March 1961) was, until its departure, still referred in diplomatic dispatches under the outmoded designation of '*Ambassadeur aux Indes* (Indies)' and not as '*Ambassadeur en Inde* (India)' which became the convention only with his successor.

THE DEBILITATING COLONIAL FACTOR

Bilateral relations between France and India started even before 15 August 1947. The exchange of diplomatic missions at the embassy level was officially announced on 17 February 1947, just a few days before the British prime minister, Clement Atlee, declared his government's intention to handover the entire responsibility and power to a competent Indian authority by June 1948. Jawaharlal Nehru, who wanted to obtain international recognition as early as possible—especially from the five permanent members of the United Nations Security Council—had made it clear that France should be represented at the highest level in New Delhi.[3] The United States and China had already upgraded their diplomatic representation in the Indian capital. Christian Fouchet, Consul General of France in Calcutta, announced on 29 January 1947 that the French authorities had agreed to the reciprocal opening of embassies just a few days after informing Nehru that the French government was only willing to open immediately 'something that resembled a legation' in view of the provisional nature of the interim government in India.[4] France found itself in a delicate position. It could not refuse the Indian prime minister's request, even if it meant calling "embassy" an establishment, which did not have either the structure or the objective of an embassy. Furthermore, it was important for France to establish an interaction at the highest level with India and obtain the goodwill of the Indian leadership vis-à-vis the French territories in Asia by following a policy of rapprochement and mutual understanding.[5]

It was understood from the very beginning that the colonial issue would dominate the relations between France and India. The constitution of an interim government in early September 1946 having Pandit Nehru at its head, had already made the Quai d'Orsay wonder whether it was not the right time to open an 'active and effective diplomatic mission' in India. There were three main reasons in favour of such a step. The first two reasons were based on the desire of the French to win over the Indian nationalists. They were afraid that the Indian nationalistic fervour would affect 'the fate of our establishments in India which depend mainly on our relations with Delhi' and spread to other French possessions given 'the proximity of Indo-China and the appeal of the Indian political movement to the neighbouring indigenous peoples'. The only pro-active element was 'the possibility of developing trade exchanges which the present government seems to approve for political reasons'.[6] The French colonial politics certainly did not appeal to the Indian government. Nehru admitted this to the Consul General and remarked that one reason 'for the new anxiety of the French Government to establish relations with us is this very Vietnam affair. In spite of this, however, we cannot refuse the offer. That would be an insult to a major nation.'[7] It is true that the situation in Vietnam had severely deteriorated after the bombardment of the port city of Haiphong by the French army in November 1946 and the Vietminh's retaliatory actions in Hanoi the following month. When the war started in Indo-China, it was very important for French military aircraft to have permission to overfly Indian territory with transit facilities in Delhi and Calcutta on their way from Karachi to Rangoon. The only other alternative was to make a long detour via Trincomalee.[8]

Undoubtedly, India's diplomatic activism and its solidarity with other freedom movements in Asia were a cause for worry. The first instructions given by the Asia-Oceania Office on 26 March 1947 to the first French Chargé d'Affaires, Henri Roux, said, 'the questions that should claim your immediate attention are India's attitude towards the political developments within the French Union, especially in Indo-China and in the French establishments in India'. It was obviously a matter of concern for the Quai d'Orsay that during international conferences, Indian representatives rarely shared the viewpoint of their French colleagues, especially in matters related to non-autonomous territories, 'where India has systematically supported views that are the most hostile to colonial powers. Because of that, the feeling has arisen that there is a basic antagonism between the policies of France and India. It is mainly this feeling that you must try to dispel.' It was hoped that the French Chargé d'Affaires' task would become easier if the Indian leaders took a more moderate stand once the country became fully independent. There was no need for France to be ashamed about its presence overseas in its dealings with the Indians, who were known to be sensitive to questions related to racial segregation. It was enough to remind them of the 'humanitarian principles that had inspired the colonial policy of the Third Republic' and that 'the idea of racial discrimination and prejudice against coloured people had always been alien to the spirit of the French people'.[9]

It was only a matter of convincing the Indians that the partnership pacts that France wanted to sign with the countries of Indo-China did not in any way deny 'the right to complete independence for the peoples of Indo-China', keeping in mind, nevertheless, that the latter still lacked political maturity. France's willingness to set Indo-China on the road to emancipation was the first point of the strategy devised to answer India's objections. The second point was to discredit the Vietminh by drawing attention to the totalitarian methods it employed to force itself on the people of Vietnam, methods that were far removed from 'Pandit Nehru's political doctrines that are closer to Gandhi's ideology of non-violence than to those of Moscow'. As for the French settlements in India, a lot of hope was placed in Nehru's repeated statements that India wanted to make Pondicherry 'a window open to the West'. Paris therefore strove to convince the Indian government 'to naturally consider Pondicherry and, by extension, our four other "establishments" in India as enjoying a special status that would allow us to maintain our rights there'.[10]

While Paris was sending these instructions to its representative in India, the first Asian Relations Conference was being held in the Indian capital. Nehru declared during the conference that it was an anachronism that Asian countries should be ruled from European capitals. The Indian prime minister believed that the quick and friendly return of French settlements (Chandernagore, Karaikal, Mahe, Pondicherry, Yanam) to India, justified a softening of the Indian stand towards the France's Indo-China policy, apart from the fact that the Communist leaders of Vietnam's anti-colonial movement did not necessarily find favour with Delhi. Also, Paris noted with satisfaction that though the conference had provided a platform for Vietminh propaganda, 'Pandit Nehru intervened personally to prevent the Vietnamese delegation from attacking France and, all said and done, our country was not treated any worse than England, Holland and even the United States.'[11]

Apart from these settlements, French possessions in India also included trading posts called 'loges' on the sites of the factories of the French East India Company.[12] Negotiations for their surrender had already been initiated in 1945, but did not lead to any concrete results. In the spring of 1947, the Indian Minister of External Affairs unofficially asked that these territories be surrendered voluntarily to India as a sign of goodwill. In a letter dated 12 August 1947, Georges Bidault announced to the Indian prime minister the French government's decision to cede its historical rights on the 'loges' to the Dominion of India. This became a reality on 6 October 1947. In any case, French authority over these 'loges' had been rather tenuous, if not non-existent. To repeat the words of a note written by the Office for Political Affairs in the French ministry of Foreign Affairs, at that point of time these 'loges' represented no more than 'the scattered tiny crumbs of a wonderful slice of history'.[13] The official announcement of the transfer of the 'loges' was for France a genuine proof of its conciliatory attitude and its desire to get in favour with the Indian prime minister rather than face a flare-up in the French territories in India as 15 August drew nearer. This decision was a prelude to the joint declaration of 27 August 1947 by which the two governments decided to study in common, 'ways and means of a friendly regulation of the problems of French establishments in India, with due regard to the interests and aspirations of the population of these territories, to the historical and cultural links of these people with France and to the evolution of India'.[14]

During the next seven years, the future of France's presence in India was linked with its presence in Indo-China. In the first place, for its war effort in Indo-China to continue unabated, the French government had to depend on the Indian government's benevolent attitude for transit and refuelling facilities. In November 1947, the Indian government refused to accede to a French request for an increase in the number of overflights of its military planes transporting equipment or personnel to Indo-China that could prolong the conflict and lead 'to the suppression of the national aspirations of the people of Vietnam'.[15] The Indian government, which did not want to appear to be supporting the French war effort in Vietnam, seemed only willing to adhere to a Anglo-French agreement of March 1947 allowing a monthly quota of eight aeroplanes. The only exceptions admissible to the Indian ministry of External Affairs were hospital planes and aircraft carrying civil or medical personnel.

When Chargé d'Affaires Henri Roux noticed an apparent hardening of the Indian stand regarding military air links with Indo-China, he suggested that the only solution was to start negotiations in a liberal spirit and as soon as possible to decide the future of French settlements in India. 'If we decide to make the gesture that New Delhi expects of us, we may perhaps obtain in return from the Indian authorities that they will turn a blind eye on the passage of some military and transport planes on their way to Indo-China. The local opinion could not, if we were to relinquish our sovereignty over our five settlements, accuse us of imperialism and colonialism in India and we would be favourably considered which may modify, to a certain extent, the ill feelings that our action in Indo-China generates'. He finally declared that there was no point in waiting because 'our settlements will gradually break away from us in any case, but without allowing us to obtain in return for their loss advantages that a voluntary surrender would gain for us today'.[16] The plenipotentiary Minister and Chargé d'Affaires finally suggested that Pondicherry should be surrendered to save Saigon. However, the government in Paris, more particularly the Ministry for Overseas Territories, had no intention of giving in on either of the two fronts.

On 15 June 1948, a treaty was formally signed between India and France for holding municipal elections in Chandernagore, Pondicherry, Karaikal, Mahe and Yanam for electing municipal councillors who would hold a referendum to decide the future status of these settlements. Elections took place in Chandernagore in August 1948 leading to the victory of councillors who favoured accession to India. The referendum held in June 1949 confirmed the unwillingness of the people of Chandernagore to continue as a part of the French Union. On the contrary, in Pondicherry, Karaikal and Yanam, where elections were held in October 1948 (and in Mahe in February 1949), the candidates opposed to accession to India were generally the winners. Nehru remained patient in the expectation that the problem of French and Portuguese possessions would be resolved by itself in the course of time in India's favour. However, his wait-and-watch policy did not always go down well with the other members of his government, particularly the Home Minister, Sardar Patel, militant elements in the Congress party and even more so with the public opinion to whom a referendum to determine the future of these territories seemed superfluous. As for Indo-China, even though the Indian prime minister still refused to recognize the Vietminh, he doubted whether the Bao-Dai government really mirrored the nationalist anti-Communist elements. New Delhi was not fooled by the powers granted by the French government to the former emperor of Annam and it had no intention of giving official recognition to the Bao-Dai regime installed as a result of the Along Bay agreements signed in June 1948, or to any of the other associated states of Indo-China, on the grounds that the transfer of powers did not go far enough.

The negotiations on the future of the French settlements failed to make any progress. So in 1952, the Indian government denounced the 1948 agreement providing for a referendum and demanded a pure and simple surrender. The argument they put forward was that conditions were no longer favourable for holding an honest plebiscite. Reading between the lines, it was evident that India did not want to set a precedent that could be applied to Kashmir.[17] Relations between Paris and New Delhi deteriorated as seen in a dispatch dated March 1952, in which Ambassador Ostrorog could not but take note of the isolation of France in India, comparable to that of Portugal and South Africa. This was unnecessarily prejudicial since 'France is on another level . . . it still has enough potential to renew and revive her action, adapt it to circumstances, act effectively instead of hanging on to things that are beyond resurrection' (like the treaty ceding Chandernagore which was still not ratified). For the French Ambassador, the least that France could do was to agree to an amicable solution of the problem of the settlements.[18] All the more so because the developments in Tunisia and Morocco were being followed with interest in India. Nehru received Bourguiba in March 1951 and the Neo-Dastur opened an office in the Indian capital in early 1953. India sided with the Arab countries in asking the United Nations to examine the Moroccan and Tunisian questions. Besides a genuine anti-colonialism, this step was also a part of India's efforts vis-à-vis the Arab countries not to yield ground to Pakistan in the defence of Muslim countries. In July 1952, on noticing a further deterioration of France's relations with Nehru, Ostrorog observed that 'what can attract him to France are the principles of 1789 and our liberal vocation. He believes that we have distanced ourselves from this ideal at present and, as our relations with him have been practically suspended, we can do nothing to make him change his opinion.'[19]

In this respect, 1954 was a promising year for Indo-French relations. Even if France did oppose India's participation in the Geneva Conference, the armistice in Indo-China was concluded in July and India was elected chairman of the International Supervisory Commissions entrusted with the task of implementing the Geneva agreements. Spurred on by the new French prime minister, Pierre Mendès France, the threads of dialogue were taken up again in Tunisia. Finally, an agreement on the *de facto* transfer of the French settlements to the Indian Union was signed on 21 October 1954 after France gave up the idea of holding a plebiscite. By a singular twist of fate, the Indian government took over the administration of the French territories on 1 November 1954, the very same day Algeria witnessed the beginning of another anti-colonial uprising. The annual report on 1954 of the French Embassy in New Delhi displayed a certain amount of optimism. It observed that since France could not expect any sympathy from the Soviet Union and since it did not have any relations with the People's Republic of China, it had no other option but to come to an understanding with India for giving substance to an Asian policy. 'Otherwise, we will have to admit that we lack the means and that we have only enemies in Asia. . . . After years of fruitless opposition, there is a rapprochement that could become stronger with time and make things easier in the future.' Further, by cooperating with India, France would be in a better position to defend its position in Indo-China 'in the face of Chinese advances in Laos, the strong hold of the United States over Cambodia and the assistance provided by the Vietminh to the Pathet-Lao in violation of the Geneva agreements'.[20]

The fact that India used moderate terms while referring to France during the Bandung Conference in the spring of 1955 did not pass unnoticed. After the SEATO Conference in Karachi in March 1956, the French Foreign Minister, Christian Pineau, visited New Delhi. It was the first visit to India by a leading French official, while Nehru, who was very familiar with the French capital, had visited Paris the previous month. During two long meetings, Christian Pineau and the Indian prime minister covered the entire gamut of political issues. They agreed on several points, especially that it was the right time to give some credit to the new Soviet leaders for trying to establish grounds for coexistence. Progress in the field of decolonialization had improved the atmosphere. France's refusal to join the Baghdad Pact, contrary to Great Britain, was considered a point in favour of Paris and the return of the Socialists to power in France under the leadership of Guy Mollet provided *a priori* interlocutors with whom Nehru could get along. Thus, of all the leading European countries at that time, France seemed to be the closest to India in terms of political views. And though he deplored the bloodshed in Algeria, the Indian prime minister did not dispute the intractability of the problem and the necessity of finding a solution that would be acceptable to both sections of the population. The Quai d'Orsay took note that the Indian government had refrained from associating itself with the demand of the Arab-Asian group that the Algerian question should figure on the UN agenda.[21] The signature in Delhi, on 28 May 1956, of the French establishments cessation treaty confirmed the new warmth of Indo-French relations.

But the Suez affair changed the situation completely. The Anglo-French intervention was described as a return to inadmissible colonial behaviour in the Near East. When Nehru stated in an interview on the Canadian television that the situation in Algeria was no better than the situation in Hungary, the President of the Council summoned the Indian Ambassador in France, K.M. Panikkar, and reminded him that at no time had the French leaders voiced their views on India's internal matters in public and never had they used such a harsh language. At the same time, he also mentioned the Kashmir issue that had been the subject of several UN resolutions that India had not followed up. India was reminded that France, on the contrary, had complied with the resolutions passed by the UN General Assembly regarding the Suez affair, no matter what the cost.[22] The French stand on Kashmir, when the question was debated in the UN (in 1952, 1957, 1962, 1964), consisted in theory of avoiding taking sides with either of the two contending parties, notably on the grounds that it was a matter that concerned first and foremost the Commonwealth. This official attempt to maintain a balance brought France praises as well as reproaches from both India and Pakistan, depending on whether a declaration was interpreted a tilt in favour of one side or the other. On one instance, Zulfikar Ali Bhutto, the then Pakistani Foreign Minister, in a meeting in Paris with its French counterpart, Maurice Couve de Murville, complained that the French representative in the Security Council, Roger Seydoux, had declared in February 1964 that any solution to the Kashmir issue should also take into account 'the legitimate interests of both parties'. The Indian side had then read these words as contradicting the self-determination principle that France had till then supported and as weakening the claim for plebiscite.[23] Two months later, it was the turn of the Indian Embassy in Paris to protest against a recent declaration of the same French representative in which he favoured a pro-active role for the United Nations, to Pakistan's satisfaction.[24] Actually, the basic French position could be seen on the whole as more favourable to Pakistan because, like all Western powers, Paris supported the right of self-determination of the Kashmiri people by holding, if the need arose, a plebiscite under the auspices of the UN. France therefore showed a certain amount of irritation towards what it believed was India's intransigence. Paris was also constrained by the fact that Pakistan was a member of Western alliances. These considerations decided France's stand when the matter was put to vote in the UN.

As for Pakistan, it did not hide the fact in the early 1950s that it was generally satisfied with the stand taken by Paris regarding Kashmir. It did not, therefore, intend to create difficulties for France regarding the colonial problem although there were occasional demonstrations of Muslim solidarity in support of independence for Tunisia and Morocco. In fact, the controversy about the French and Portuguese settlements in India was a boon for Karachi because it showed the international community that the process of integration was not yet complete within the Indian Union. Pakistan was certainly thinking of Kashmir and it fully appreciated the initial insistence of France on holding a referendum before deciding on the transfer of its settlements to India.

FORM WITHOUT SUBSTANCE

The circumstances that brought General de Gaulle to power in France in 1958 were not to Nehru's liking, as the Indian prime minister was averse to heads of state with a military background. De Gaulle, for his part, did not like the way India laid its hands on the French settlements in 1954, calling it an 'inadmissible act of brutality'.[25] If we were to believe Sarvepalli Gopal, Nehru's best-known biographer, the latter was almost convinced that de Gaulle had fulfilled his historical destiny with the liberation of France and that 'against his better judgement, (he) had a tendency to compare the General to Mussolini rather than Churchill'.[26] For all that, the two leaders were of the same age, Nehru having been born in 1889 and the General in 1890. Though they did not share the same ideological convictions—Nehru being a socialist—they were both equally concerned about national independence and the international status of their respective countries, even if the methods employed to reach this goal were different. The first person who was given the task of disabusing Nehru about the true nature of General de Gaulle was André Malraux. He visited India in November 1958 in the course of a journey in Asia that also took him to Iran and Japan. Though the two men knew and respected each other, they did not always share the same concerns. Malraux stressed India's unique place among the great civilizations of the world, its unequalled spiritual contribution which could be the basis of a new world and that because of this legacy, as well as Gandhi's inspiration and Nehru's action, it had based its policy on a moral concept. But while Malraux harped on spiritual values, Nehru insisted on the immediate need of solving the material problems of India's poverty-stricken masses.[27]

There was no reference to immediate political problems during these discussions. The Indian prime minister continued to believe that the test of de Gaulle's success or failure would rest on his handling of the Algerian problem, which affected not only India's foreign policy but also its interests.[28] The Indian leaders, whose sympathies naturally lay with any movement for political independence, were also worried about the opinion of Arab nations as well as the general sentiment prevailing in Afro-Asian countries. However, New Delhi's attitude regarding the Algerian question was always tempered by moderation, despite the outbursts of Krishna Menon, the leader of the Indian delegation to the United Nations. This delegation tried nonetheless to generally tone down the violent attacks launched against France by countries belonging to the Bandung group. In November 1958, the Indian prime minister, who favoured an amicable solution acceptable to all parties, sent a message to Nasser asking him to use his influence with the leaders of the National Liberation Front (FLN) to get them to accept the invitation extended by the French government to visit Paris. Although the FLN had opened an office in Delhi in the summer of 1957, which was subsidised by the Congress party, the Indian government did not officially recognize the provisional government of Ferhat Abbas even though he visited Delhi in 1959. During a meeting with General de Gaulle in Paris on 8 May 1960, just before the 'Big Four' Conference, the Indian prime minister indicated his approval of the official policy of self-determination for the Algerian people. About this meeting, Nehru had mixed feelings. He was taken aback by de Gaulle's imperious ways, gathering the impression that, 'one does not speak with de Gaulle, one listens. He did not seem to expect much from me', adding he had also 'the impression that the General does not expect anything from anyone'. Nehru was by then rather well disposed towards the man who had given independence to many French African colonies and he was indeed favourably impressed by the strength of its convictions and its long-term vision. 'It indeed made me feel younger, even if we both were seventy years old', commenting also that 'listening to him made you feel as if we still had a long way to go.' Nevertheless, as the Algerian war lingered on as well as the ratification by the French parliament of the treaty surrendering the French settlements in India, a feeling of impatience crept over the Indian prime minister. Nehru was also put off by de Gaulle's disregard for the UN which unveiled a lack of concern for the attachment of the young nation-states to it and shown an 'outdated belief that everything should be worked out by the Big Powers and that everything is ruled by confrontation'.[29]

Two things may have eventually contributed to refrain India from being more vocal about these disappointments. On the one hand, there was the Kashmir question mentioned earlier, on which Paris had a less antagonistic stand than the United States or the United Kingdom. On the other hand, the country was going through financial difficulties and needed external assistance for funding its five-year plans and France, though not a major economic partner, could not be fully ignored. The economic and technical cooperation treaty signed in January 1958 did not include any loans, only a simple promise to facilitate the financing of equipment imported from France up to a limit of 25 billion francs. France joined the Aid India Consortium (AIC) in 1961 at the beginning of India's third five-year plan (1961-6). The consortium, since its creation in 1958, consisted of Canada, Federal Republic of Germany, Japan, United Kingdom, United States as well as the International Bank for Reconstruction and Development and the International Monetary Fund. France's role among the countries helping India was relatively small (French bilateral aid, which was earlier non-existent, amounted to a little over 2 per cent of the foreign aid sanctioned by the AIC during the third five-year plan). The Quai d'Orsay was aware that in view of the existing commitments towards other underdeveloped countries, especially the African countries, it could not but play a limited role in the international effort to help India. However, it also believed that its absence 'during a period of accelerated development, in which all developed countries were taking part, was likely to create a situation that would be unfavourable not only for our economic expansion but also for our political influence all over Asia'.[30]

When he was requested once again by the provisional government of the Algerian Republic (*Gouvernement Provisoire de la République Algérienne* = GPRA) during the first conference of the Non-Aligned Movement in Belgrade in September 1961, Nehru did not want to follow the example set by other countries (Afghanistan, Ghana, Cambodia and Yugoslavia) that had taken advantage of this event to publicly announce their *de jure* recognition of the GPRA. The Indian government waited until Algeria became independent in July 1962 to announce its recognition. This benevolent attitude had indeed contrasted with Pakistan's recognition of the GPRA and this could not have been overseen when the Kashmir issue was again taken up at the UN by the Security Council in the spring of 1962. 'If Pakistan is our ally within SEATO, its behaviour in the Algerian affair has not been as friendly as we hoped for' was explained in a telegram sent by the Quai d'Orsay to the French representative at the UN. 'Furthermore, if the Indian argument is open to criticism, it is our interest to treat India tactfully since it had a more correct attitude concerning Algeria and that we wish, after the ratification of the cession agreements of our former establishments, to reach a friendly agreement over its delicate mode of enforcement.'[31] The French government under Michel Debré had to yield to political compulsions that supported a final solution of the Indo-French dispute and he had tabled a bill seeking the ratification of the treaty on 15 December 1961. Once the Foreign Affairs Committee of the National Assembly had backed the bill, it was put on the agenda of the French parliament session on 12 July 1962 when it was passed after a relatively peaceful debate. The instruments of ratification were exchanged subsequently in New Delhi on 16 August 1962.

Once the colonial issue, which had severely affected the relations between India and France, became a thing of the past, a cordial and enduring cooperation between the two countries could really take roots. Even more so because France was less exposed to criticism than the United States and the United Kingdom. For instance, their outcry against the purchase by India of Soviet Mig-21 fighter planes to India—they even encouraged at one point France to sell instead Mirage IV fighters at a price financially acceptable to New Delhi—made the Indian leadership bristle. Nehru and de Gaulle met for the last time in September 1962. The European Common Market and its eventual repercussions on India (especially if the United Kingdom decided to join it), Indo-China and the Sino-Indian border dispute figured among the topics discussed by the two leaders. The personal relationship between them continued to be lukewarm even though there were no political differences between their countries, which prompted Nehru to express the wish that India and France would strengthen their economic and cultural collaboration substantially.[32] India's Ambassador, Ali Yavar Jung commented that France 'has the advantage in India's eyes of being an economically and financially sound country and at the same time level-headed without being a "compromising" power like USSR or the United States'. Besides, New Delhi believed that the French government's views on questions like Asia's neutrality, particularly with reference to the countries of Indo-China, were similar to its own.[33] At the time the Indian ambassador was making this statement, India had already entered into a war with China.

Right from the beginning of the conflict, which started on 20 October 1962, Nehru clarified India's intention to obtain the arms needed for its defence from any country willing to supply them. The United States and the United Kingdom agreed at the end of October to organize an airlift to deliver infantry equipment for the Himalayan battle-front. Other countries, especially France, Australia, Canada, Japan, Israel and the Federal Republic of Germany declared that they were ready to supply arms, ammunition and other equipments either in the form of grants or on credit. Close cooperation had developed between the defence services of India and France. For instance, just few months before the war, a contract for the sale of Alouette III helicopters had been signed with the right to manufacture under licence. Negotiations were carried out for the supply of military equipment amounting to more than 20 billion francs (mortars, AMX tanks, helicopters, spare parts for Mystère and Ouragan fighter planes, shells, etc.). Nehru wrote to de Gaulle on 13 December 1962, requesting his personal intervention for a financial arrangement for deferred payment or payment in rupees. While other Western countries showed generosity, India was disappointed by the financial conditions imposed by the French (cash payment on delivery and credit periods that were considered too short) even though France provided spare parts worth 4 million dollars free of cost for its Ouragan fighter planes.

De Gaulle was already thinking of recognizing the People's Republic of China. Edgar Faure, former President of the Council was sent on an exploratory mission to Beijing in October 1963. On his return journey, he stopped in New Delhi for talks with the Indian leaders. India had for a long time fought for the admission of the People's Republic of China to the United Nations so that it was not isolated from the rest of the world, which was considered a situation fraught with danger. Normally, India should have been happy that China had finally been recognized by France (recognition was given in January 1964). But now India was concerned of a shift in France's economic and political policy in favour of China to the detriment of its policy of cooperation with the Indian Union. The trauma of its defeat by China in 1962 would be transferred to the Vietnamese question according to a diplomatic assessment. Like France, New Delhi was officially in favour of a united and neutral Vietnam, but in reality confronted by the Chinese threat, which a victory for North Vietnam would only exacerbate, it valued the presence of American troops in the Indo-China peninsula, without actually admitting it.[34]

Georges Pompidou's visit to India in February 1965, the first visit by a French prime minister (it is only in January 1980 that a French head of State, Valery Giscard d'Estaing, paid a state visit to India), was an occasion to remind each other that there was more outward show than substance in the similarity of their positions. When de Gaulle and Nehru met in September 1962, the French President had pointed out that France did not think it desirable that the UN should become militarily involved in Congo and hence disapproved of the presence of Indian troops in the UN forces. Nehru had then replied that the UN action in Congo was necessary to avoid the dismemberment of the country and civil war. As for disarmament, France had centred its policy of independence on nuclear deterrence and followed a 'vacant seat' policy at the Eighteen-Nation Disarmament Committee, which had begun its works in Geneva in March 1962. If by then the atomic energy agencies of the two countries had been cooperating for many years (the first agreement was signed in 1951) and many Indian scientists had gone to Saclay for training (Homi Bhabha died in a plane crash in the Alps while going to Paris to attend one of those regular meetings with French counterparts), France and India had divergent positions regarding the military uses of nuclear energy. New Delhi lend its support to the Moscow Partial Test Ban Treaty of August 1963, banning all but underground nuclear tests. France, who was conducting tests in the Sahara, had refused to sign the treaty since it considered it a sham. Krishna Menon had been virulently critical in the UN of the French nuclear test in May 1962. With the passage of time, India was to become less vocal when it came to condemning French tests and it was interpreted as a sure sign that India was determined to keep the nuclear option open. The French Ambassador, in July 1972, wrote that India could conduct, in the more or less near future, underground nuclear experiments in the Thar Desert.[35]

The Ambassador of France in India, Jean-Paul Garnier, was thus able to say that 'though General de Gaulle's authority and the prestige he enjoys in the Third World are deeply felt here . . . the Indian and French policies follow separate paths, sometimes parallel but never convergent. They do not clash however and it is ultimately this absence of opposition—because there is no meeting point—between our forces that seems to be the basis of our good relations.'[36] France's stand at the time of the Indo-Pakistan war of September 1965 was generally appreciated. Paris opposed any references to the idea of sanctions imposed by the UN on both countries and was to allow in November the sale of spare parts for Mirage IV which contrasted with the embargo imposed by the United States and the United Kingdom. Nevertheless the French diplomacy did support the idea that a ceasefire agreement concluded under the auspices of the UN should also contemplate steps towards instigating negotiations getting to the root of the problem. This was hardly acceptable to India, who considering itself as the aggrieved party in the conflict, was opposed to any implicit link between a ceasefire and an international mediation on Kashmir. If pessimism over a breakthrough was shared by Paris and New Delhi, the way of looking at the solution was certainly not convergent. If the Quai d'Orsay thought that a solution to the Kashmir question could of course come through a direct understanding between the parties, this was highly problematic and more likely a solution would come 'through the intervention of concerned big powers within the framework of the Security Council or otherwise, i.e. following a compromise acceptable to India and Pakistan or even strongly advised. Now an international solution mapped out with the United Nations seems doubtful in the absence of China, affected in particular by its geographical proximity as the evolution of events have amply demonstrated: the conclusion of border agreements with Pakistan in 1963 and 1965, the ultimatum addressed to India in September.'[37]

A few weeks after Indira Gandhi took over as the prime minister after the sudden death of Lal Bahadur Shastri in January 1966 during the Tashkent Conference, she met General de Gaulle while she was passing through Paris on her way to America. Few days earlier, in an act of defiance appealing to a non-aligned country opposed to military pacts, the French President had written to Lyndon Johnson to inform him that France, while remaining a member of NATO, will no longer assign its forces to it and that it will withdraw from the integrated military structure with the consequence that allied forces and NATO headquarters must move out of the country. De Gaulle, in a avuncular tone, advised Nehru's daughter, who did not hide her distrust of her Pakistani and Chinese neighbours, to 'support Pakistan (who) will never do you much harm and does not represent an excessively important factor for you'. He felt that the highly ambitious China would be harder to deal with. Nevertheless, 'for the next thirty years, you can rest assured that it will not willingly go to war . . . because it needs about thirty years to attain its full strength, and the same holds true for you'. Before concluding on a reassuring note, 'your external situation is therefore not serious and you are not threatened with disappearance', de Gaulle went so far as to find some similarity between the positions of France and India. He claimed that to be heard it would be in their interest to distance themselves from the game played by the three world powers, viz., the United States, China and Russia.[38] The possibility of a nuclear non-proliferation treaty would once again lead to a confrontation between French and Indian views. Both the countries agreed on one point—their refusal to sign the treaty was based on an official line of reasoning that was quite similar. In the face of a discriminatory treaty, France refused to pressurise other countries to give up their nuclear option, refusing nevertheless to assist third countries that would be tempted to develop a nuclear arsenal. Short of a total ban on nuclear armaments, there was little doubt that other countries would ultimately acquire them. India, for its part, was opposed to all non-proliferation that was not both horizontal and vertical, to inspections imposed on non-nuclear powers without any assurance of reciprocity and to the inability of the latter to conduct underground tests for 'peaceful' purposes. If going nuclear was hence not a closed option as a non-signatory of the NPT, India was officially opposed to exercising the option and, not being a member of any alliance or any system of collective security, wanted in return for its restraint a guarantee from the nuclear powers that they would come to its help if it had to face any nuclear blackmail. This was the assurance that L.K. Jha, Secretary to the prime minister, wanted when he visited Paris in the spring of 1967 after having been to Moscow, Washington and London. However, there was no formal commitment.

Regarding the Bangladesh liberation war, France tried to have essentially a moderating influence. France recognized Bangladesh in February 1972. India seemed to have been satisfied with the French position since an informal approach was made to see if France would be ready to sign a treaty of friendship with India. This approach was interpreted as an attempt by New Delhi, after the Indo-Soviet treaty of August 1971, to reassert its non-alignment. But the Indian offer was not taken up for multiple reasons: the first one being that France during the last few years had only signed a bilateral treaty of such significance with West Germany, a treaty which served as a cornerstone for the French European policy. Second, France was not a big power in Asia comparable to the Soviet Union, China or Japan. To sign a treaty with India would mean interfering too much in Asian affairs, siding with India and taking the risk of offending countries with whom India had difficult relations, viz., China and Pakistan. Third reason, the situation in the subcontinent had not been fully stabilized and France did not want to appear as favouring one side. Nevertheless, France was conscious that India's power had increased in Asia after the war with Pakistan and that France had every interest to see India asserting its power, if non-expansionist, so as to participate of the balance of power in Asia.[39]

Conclusion

It is necessary to differentiate two periods in the history of Indo-French relations between 1947 and 1972. The first period starting from the time India became independent and ending in the late 1950s was dominated by the colonial issue. India was then seen as a potentially antagonistic country because of its anti-colonial stance, although it must be admitted that Nehru, who ranked France and its culture very high in his humanistic world-view, showed a great deal of understanding as regards the compulsions of French politics. In a note portraying the Indian prime minister written on the day of his death on 27 May 1964, the Quai d'Orsay said, 'Nobody was undoubtedly happier than him to see the relations between our two countries moving finally, after so many vicissitudes, towards a cordial cooperation of which he was certainly the main architect on the Indian side.'[40] Non-aligned India could not but support the Gaullist government's desire to remain independent of the two power blocs. This viewpoint was reflected in a dispatch from the new French Ambassador in India, Jean Daridan, at the end of 1965. He said that the Indian leaders were very keen of finding an interlocutor in Europe and that because of its policy and the personality of its president, this interlocutor could be none other than France. 'Neither Great Britain, which is held in great distrust, nor the Federal Republic of Germany considered to be too subservient to the United States could play this role. The leaders in Delhi expect advice and support from us.'[41] On the French side, de Gaulle was to write in *Mémoires d'Espoir* that 'France, as a champion of the balance of power, has the best raisons to wish that, facing China, Hindustan assert its capabilities'.[42] If there were any expectations from Indian diplomacy in recognition of the originality of French foreign policy, they were fulfilled at a time when India was passing through excruciating times in the wake of the 1962 Sino-Indian conflict compounded by economic difficulties and had consequently little room for manoeuvre on the international scene. This limited the scope for a constructive partnership.

NOTES

1. From Archibald Nye, United Kingdom High Commissioner, to the Secretary of State for Commonwealth Relations, 17 May 1951. *Public Record Office*, FO 371 92870.
2. Rajeshwar Dayal, *A Life of Our Times*, New Delhi: Orient Longman, 1998, p. 567.
3. Nehru's note to Georges Bidault, 10 December 1946. Sarvepalli Gopal (gen. ed.), *Selected Works of Jawaharlal Nehru, Second Series*, vol. 1, New Delhi: Jawaharlal Nehru Memorial Fund, 1984, p. 552. V.K. Krishna Menon was asked to hand this note personally to G. Bidault.
4. Letter to V.K. Krishna Menon, 13 January 1947, Ibid., p. 563.
5. From the Minister of External Affairs to the Ambassador of France in London, 24 January 1947. *Archives du Quai d'Orsay, Asie-Océanie*, 1944-1955, *Inde*, vol. 62.
6. Note from the *Direction Asie-Océanie*, 8 November 1946, Ibid.
7. Letter to V.K. Krishna Menon, 29 January 1947. Sarvepalli Gopal (gen. ed.), *Selected Works of Jawaharlal Nehru, Second Series*, vol. 1, pp. 586-7.
8. There was a saving of almost a thousand kilometres (Karachi–Delhi 1120 km, Delhi–Calcutta 1325 km and Calcutta–Rangoon 1100 km) as compared to the route via Trincomalee (Karachi–Trincomalee approx. 2700 km and Trincomalee–Rangoon 1900 km in a zone where weather conditions are often bad).
9. In his message dated 5 February 1947 addressed to Georges Bidault, Nehru thanked the French delegation at the United Nations for its support during the debate on the treatment of Indians in South Africa.
10. Note from the *Direction Asie-Océanie*, 9 December 1946. *Archives du Quai d'Orsay, Asie-Océanie*, 1944-1955, *Inde*, vol. 62.
11. Telegram from the *Direction Asie-Océanie* to the embassy in Nanking and the legations in Bangkok and Saigon, 11 April 1947. Ibid. Nevertheless, it is not known for certain if Nehru really appreciated the remarks made by General Bollaert, the French High Commissioner in Indo-China, when he passed through Delhi in June 1947. He insisted that there would be trouble if France failed in its civilizing mission by abandoning Vietnam to a totalitarian party whose methods consisted of suppressing democracy and individual freedom.
12. The 'loges' covered an area of 285 ha whereas the French settlements covered around 500 sq. km with a population of 360,000 of whom 270,000 were French nationals. France's rights on these 'loges' were established by the treaties of 30 May 1814 and 20 November 1815. After the Napoleonic wars, the British government had agreed under these treaties to return to France the different types of settlements and trading posts it had in Asia as of 1 January 1792.
13. Note on the 'loges' in the Indian peninsula, 20 December 1949, Ibid., vol. 28.

14. *Foreign Policy of India: Text of Documents 1947-59*. New Delhi, Lok Sabha Secretariat, 1959, p. 3.
15. This refusal was directly related to the overflight by two Halifax military aircraft and followed another refusal to permit small battleships to put in at Cochin. Dispatch from Henri Roux, 21 November 1947. *Archives du Quai d'Orsay, Asie-Océanie*, 1944-1955, *Inde*, vol. 62. France's first Ambassador to India, Daniel Levi, son of well-known Indologist Sylvain Levi, took up his post in December 1947.
16. Ibid. It should be noted that on 24 December 1948, India, together with Pakistan and Sri Lanka, decided to stop the overflight of aeroplanes belonging to the Dutch airline KLM following the escalation of the conflict in Indonesia.
17. According to a British diplomat, 'Manac'h [the Director for Asian Affairs at the Quai d'Orsay] made an interesting comment on the change in the Indian attitude to self-determination. He said that, before handing over Pondicherry, the French government had informed the Indians that they were required by the Constitution to consult all French citizens by means of a plebiscite. The Indians opposed this on the grounds that it would constitute a precedent for a plebiscite in Kashmir. Accordingly, it was only possible to consult the *conseillers municipaux* and, as the requirements of the French constitution were not met, the territory was never formally ceded.' From H.A.F. Hohler (Paris) to E. Bolland (FO): Talk with *Directeur d'Asie* (Manac'h) on 13/10/65, 14 October 1965. *Public Record Office*, FO 371 180964.
18. Dispatch from Stanislas Ostrorog, 1 March 1952. *Archives du Quai d'Orsay, Asie-Océanie*, 1944-1955, *Inde*, vol. 64.
19. Dispatch from Stanislas Ostrorog, 9 July 1952. Ibid.
20. Note from the *Direction Asie-Océanie*, 27 October 1955. Ibid., vol. 65.
21. Note from the *Direction générale des affaires politiques, Asie-Océanie*, 15 July 1956. *Archives du Quai d'Orsay, Asie-Océanie*, 1956-1967, *Inde*, vol. 233.
22. Telegram from the *Bureau Asie-Océanie* for the attention of the Ambassador of France in New Delhi, 3 January 1957. Ibid., vol. 234.
23. Meeting between Z.A. Bhutto and M. Couve de Murville, 24 March 1964. *Archives du Quai d'Orsay, Nations-Unies et Organisations Internationales*, 1960-1964, S 50-2-A 14, box no. 742.
24. Note from the *Direction Asie-Océanie*, 14 May 1964. Ibid.
25. Alain Peyrefitte, *C'était de Gaulle*, vol. 2, Paris: Fayard, 1997, p. 474.
26. Sarvepalli Gopal, 'De Gaulle et Nehru', *Espoir*, no. 79, March 1992, p. 71.
27. Dispatch from Stanislas Ostrorog, 29 November 1958. *Archives du Quai d'Orsay, Asie-Océanie*, 1956-1967, *Inde*, vol. 235.
28. Jawaharlal Nehru, *Letters to Chief Ministers*, vol. 5: *1958-1964*, New Delhi: Jawaharlal Nehru Memorial Fund, 1989, p. 66.
29. Interview in New York with Jean Daniel. *L'Express*, 13 October 1960.
30. Note from the *Bureau Asie-Océanie* dated 30 March 1961. *Archives du Quai d'Orsay, Asie-Océanie*, 1956-1967, *Inde*, vol. 215.

31. Telegram of the Director for Political Affairs (Charles Lucet), 30 April 1962. *Archives du Quai d'Orsay, Nations Unies et Organisations Internationales*, 1960-1964, S 50-2-A 14, box no. 742.
32. Nehru's report on his talks with de Gaulle, 22 September 1962, Ministry of External Affairs, dossier 101/66, 6WI/62. Quoted by Sarvepalli Gopal, 'De Gaulle et Nehru', *Espoir*, no. 79, March 1992, p. 72.
33. India's Ambassador's visit to the Director for Asian affairs, 31 October 1962. *Archives du Quai d'Orsay, Asie-Océanie*, 1956-1967, *Inde*, vol. 185.
34. Note from the *Direction Asie-Océanie*, 20 September 1969. *Archives du Quai d'Orsay, Asie-Océanie*, 1968-1972, *Inde*, box no. 1635.
35. Dispatch from Jean de Lagarde, French Ambassador to India, 11 July 1972. Ibid., box no. 1636.
36. Dispatch from Jean-Paul Garnier, 2 February 1965. *Archives du Quai d'Orsay, Asie-Océanie*, 1956-1967, *Inde*, vol. 243.
37. Note from the *Direction Asie-Océanie* on the Indo-Pak conflict, 27 October 1965. *Archives du Quai d'Orsay, Nations Unies et Organisations Internationales*, 1960-1964, S 50-2-A 14, box no. 743. In the footsteps of U Thant, the United States had proposed a four-power commission, consisting of the Soviet Union, the United States, France and the United Kingdom and given the responsibility to implement the UN resolution of 20 September 1965 which ended the war. Such international commission was anathema to India and France opposed it since China would not be part of it.
38. Talks between de Gaulle and Indira Gandhi, 25 March 1966. *Archives du Quai d'Orsay, Asie-Océanie*, 1956-1967, *Inde*, vol. 245.
39. Telegram from the Ministry of Foreign Affairs to the French Ambassador in India, 28 February 1972. Note to the Minister from the *Direction Asie-Océanie*, 1 March 1972. *Archives du Quai d'Orsay, Asie-Océanie*, 1968-1972, *Inde*, box no. 1636.
40. Note from the *Direction des Affaires Politiques, Asie-Océanie*, 27 May 1964. *Archives du Quai d'Orsay, Asie-Océanie*, 1956-1967, *Inde*, vol. 241.
41. Telegram from Jean Daridan, 27 November 1965. *Archives du Quai d'Orsay Archives, Asie-Océanie*, 1956-1967, *Inde*, vol. 186. The Indian Ambassador in Paris at the time, Rajeshwar Dayal, did not say anything different when he writes in his memoirs that he 'had advised the Prime Minister of the advantage of developing close relations with a leading western European country'. This country could not be the United Kingdom since 'our ties with Britain were inevitably somewhat conditioned by memories of the past. Besides, Britain was tethered to the policies of the United States, whose interests in the Cold War it fully echoed.' On the contrary, France was the country which 'though a member of NATO, boldly chose to follow an independent line'. Rajeshwar Dayal, *A Life of Our Times*, p. 566.
42. Charles de Gaulle, *Mémoires d'espoir*, tome 1: Le renouveau (1958-1962), Paris: Plon, 1970, p. 275.

DENNIS KUX

❖ America Meets India: Jawaharlal Nehru through the Eyes of US Officials

For the first seventeen years of independence, India's foreign policy was dominated by Prime Minister Jawaharlal Nehru, who also served as his country's Foreign Minister. Even though Indian archives for this period remain closed, many of Nehru's own papers are available as well as his letters to chief ministers. These provide a good sense of Nehru's thinking and therefore the general thrust of Indian foreign policy, but, of course, lack details that only documents from the archives can offer. On the American side, all documents from the Nehru period have been declassified with extremely few exceptions. There also exists useful commentary about Nehru by senior Americans who had dealings with the Indian leader. These are the focus of this study. It begins with a discussion of US-India interaction in the years before independence and then reviews how Americans reacted to Jawaharlal Nehru.

Their reactions track fairly accurately the course of US-India relations from 1947 until 1964 when Nehru died. In the Truman years, Nehru's neutralism annoyed the Americans except for Chester Bowles, Ambassador to India in the last year of the Truman administration, who basically agreed with Nehru. In the Eisenhower years, the reaction was divided. The Secretary of State John Foster Dulles, who spearheaded the US-Pakistan alliance, strongly disagreed with the Indian leader. In contrast, President Eisenhower was far more positive although he did not understand Nehru's soft spot for the Soviet Union. His two positive encounters with Nehru in 1956 and 1959 mirrored the improvement in relations during Eisenhower's second term in the White House. The exception to this pattern came with the Kennedy administration. It was Kennedy's policy to seek better relations with India and these were achieved, especially after the United States provided military aid to help India in the border war with China in 1962. Still, President Kennedy found Nehru a great disappointment when he met with the prime minister during Nehru's visit to the United States in November 1961.

The United States and India before World War II

Before the Second World War, the United States had only limited contact with India. In the late eighteenth century, at the time when America was gaining its independence from Great Britain, India was in the early stages of becoming the jewel in the crown of the incipient British Empire. Even though the young United States government established a consulate in Calcutta in 1792, commerce with India was marginal except for the brief flourishing of the clipper ship trade during the Napoleonic era.[1] Thereafter in the remainder of the nineteenth and first part of the twentieth century, economic and other contacts were quite limited and political relations non-existent. The major American involvement and presence was through Christian missionaries who numbered only a few thousand. Indeed, roughly half of American investment in India during the 1930s, on the eve of independence, was in missionary schools, hospitals and other non-business activities.[2]

India appeared on the American radar screen only after the First World War. Mahatma Gandhi had assumed the leadership of the Indian National Congress and launched his non-violent nationalist movement for independence. Gaining widespread recognition, Gandhi was much admired. As Harold Isaacs wrote in his seminal 1958 study of American attitudes toward India and China, *Scratches on Our Mind*, 'the Gandhi image is overwhelmingly triumphant . . . He is acknowledged as a man to be admired virtually by all, whether friendly to India or hostile, attracted by Indians or repelled by them.'[3] Americans were, nonetheless, not always sure what to make of the spindly figure, part politician, part saint, wrapped in what seemed to be a bed-sheet like garment.

American liberals, especially after Franklin Roosevelt and his New Deal came to power in 1933, sympathized with India's desire for independence in keeping with the anti-imperialist tradition of the Democratic Party. Still the question never rose to national importance during the 1930s. Neither President Roosevelt nor Secretary of State Cordell Hull engaged themselves actively for the Indian cause. Far less positive, indeed downright hostile, was the India that Americans read about in Katherine Mayo's book, *Mother India*. Rather surprisingly, this blisteringly negative description of India as a squalid society with few redeeming features sold a phenomenal 256,000 copies in twenty-seven editions after it first appeared in 1927.[4]

World War II (1939-1945)

When the Second Word War began in 1939, India remained a country in the 'mysterious East' for most Americans. Images were moulded by the popular adventure stories of Rudyard Kipling and more recent exotic Hollywood movies of the British Raj. Fabulously wealthy princes, maharajahs, and suave British colonial sahibs blended in the public imagination with more somber pictures of impoverished peasants. There were further conflicting images of massive popular demonstrations for India's freedom from Britain coupled with bloody Hindu-Muslim communal disturbances. The complexities of the Hindu caste system and the problems of untouchability completed the bewildering mélange.

In contrast to 2002 when more than two million people of South Asian origin live in the United States, the 1940 census counted only a handful, some 2,400. These were mostly Sikh farmers who had migrated from the Punjab about the turn of the century to California. Unlike the current scene, where the India-American community has become prominent in the medical and information technology worlds and of late gained political influence, the Indian community before the Second World War was minuscule.

In the months immediately after Pearl Harbor, a series of shattering Allied reverses in Asia saw the Japanese wipe out European colonies in East Asia. Like tumbling dominoes, the Philippines, Malaya, Singapore, the Dutch East Indies, and Burma quickly fell to the Japanese who were threatening to invade India itself. President Franklin Roosevelt and his envoys in Delhi, Colonel Louis Johnson and William Phillips, urged the British to give India *de facto* and immediate self-government to increase Indian support for the war effort. In April 1942, Johnson became actively engaged in helping Sir Stafford Cripps' effort to shape an agreement with the Indian political parties, especially the Indian National Congress, that would ensure greater backing for the war effort.

During this process and the months that followed, Mahatma Gandhi fell out of favour with the US government. After opposing the Cripps mission, his decision to mount a Quit India movement against the British in August 1942—when the Allied cause against the Nazis and Japanese had sunk to its lowest point—seemed irrational to wartime Washington. Launching passive resistance in peacetime against the British imperialists was something that many Americans admired, but

Gandhi's call for non-cooperation with the British in the midst of the global battle against Fascism triggered a totally negative reaction among the American leaders. When the British decided to arrest Gandhi and other senior Congress leaders, neither Roosevelt nor others voiced opposition.[5]

In contrast, Roosevelt and Johnson believed that Britain had dragged its feet when Cripps was in Delhi and missed an opportunity to reach an agreement on a wartime national government with the Indian National Congress. During this period, US envoy Louis Johnson became a strong admirer of Gandhi's chief lieutenant and likely political heir, Jawaharlal Nehru. Nehru had frequent dealings with foreign journalists and became known as an articulate spokesman for a free India through these contacts and his own writings. Schooled in England, Nehru periodically visited Europe in the 1920s and 1930s but had never travelled to the United States.

Unlike Gandhi, Nehru was outspoken in his support of the Allied cause against the Germans and the Japanese. In an April 1942 cable to Roosevelt, Johnson praised Nehru as 'magnificent in cooperation with me. The President would like him and on most things they agree. . . . He is our hope here.'[6] Languishing in prison after August 1942, Nehru had no further dealings with American officials until his release in the spring of 1945 as the War was drawing to a close.

World War II brought Americans and Indians together in large numbers for the first time. More than quarter of a million American soldiers were stationed in India where the China-Burma-India (CBI) command was headquartered. The American GIs largely fulfilled engineering and supply functions and were mainly concentrated in eastern India, in Bengal and Assam, where they built airfields and other facilities for sending supplies to beleaguered Nationalist China. Their best known assignment was the highly publicized but dangerous 'over the hump' airlift that ferried supplies from India to China over the Himalayas.

After the Japanese surrender in August 1945, the American military presence in India rapidly wound down. Departing GIs sometimes became embroiled in heightened Indian domestic tensions. In February 1946, 37 Americans were among 400 hurt in riots in Calcutta that followed the conviction of an INA officer.[7] The American servicemen returned home from India with few positive memories. For most, the jungles of Assam and the slums and poverty of Calcutta erased all Hollywood images of wealth and romance. According to Harold Isaacs, the India theatre in World War II produced neither significant literature nor even motion pictures. This first substantial American encounter with India was thus almost like a passage in the night that left few lasting impressions.[8]

THE TRUMAN ADMINISTRATION (1945-1953)

Politically also, after the Labour Party defeated Winston Churchill and the Conservatives in 1945 elections, American support for India's independence was no longer needed as a prod to the British. The Labour Party had long favoured independence. What remained uncertain and delayed the British departure, were the contours of the post-Raj governmental structure. Would it be a united India as desired by the Congress? Or would there by two separate countries, a Pakistan for Muslim majority areas and an India or Hindustan for the Hindu majority parts of the British Raj, the plea of the Muslim League?

The United States played no significant role in the political discussions and negotiations that ultimately led to partition in August 1947. The US officials followed events closely, even if they did not take sides publicly in the bitter struggle between the Congress and the League. In its private assessment sent to the State Department, the US Embassy in Delhi, however, was critical of the way the Congress party managed the political negotiations and believed mistakes by its leaders bore much responsibility for the emergence of Pakistan. 'The present unhappy situation', a 22 April 1947 embassy dispatch stated,

> is as much the result of the Congress leaders' political ineptitude and lack of vision as of Mr. Jinnah's intransigence. Had Congress leaders put aside their fears regarding the effect of the Cabinet Mission plan on their party's position in Assam, the Punjab, and the Northwest Frontier Province, Mr. Jinnah would not have been provided with a logical basis for the Muslim League's current stand and India might today have been laying the ground-work for a united country instead of facing the prospect of Balkanization.[9]

When India emerged on the world stage as an independent nation in August 1947, the United States wished the new country well and assumed that given America's traditional anti-colonial stance, a friendly relationship would develop. Washington, however, saw few major US interests in South Asia and expected that the region would remain primarily within the sphere of influence of its former colonial master, the United Kingdom. American attention at the time was focused elsewhere. In Europe, the Cold War was heating up. In the Middle East, there was turmoil over Palestine and Israel. In the Far East, the principal US ally, Nationalist China, was losing ground in a civil war against its communist adversaries.

The first issue that engaged the United States diplomatically with India was the dispute over Kashmir that flared up in the autumn of 1947. The United States did not initially play a lead role in efforts to find a solution to the problem, preferring to leave this to the United Kingdom. After India brought the issue to the UN in January 1948, however, Washington inevitably began to take a more important part. At first, it (and the UN) saw a road towards a settlement of the state's future in India's suggestion that a plebiscite ultimately decide the issue of whether Kashmir become part of Pakistan or of India. In April 1948, the Security Council adopted a resolution to this effect and established the UN Commission on India and Pakistan. UNCIP was able to achieve a ceasefire in January 1949 but failed to get India and Pakistani agreement on the modalities for the plebiscite.

Kashmir was the main issue during Prime Minister Nehru's first conversation with the top levels of the US government, the meeting he had with Secretary of State George Marshall during the UN General Assembly session in Paris in October 1948. In talking with Marshall, Nehru asserted with much emotion that the fate of Kashmir was vital for India's secular democracy which he contrasted with Pakistan, a state based on religion.[10] After a separate discussion with Pakistani Prime Minister Liaquat Ali Khan, Marshall expressed little optimism about the chances for a Kashmir settlement in talking about the issue with Britain's UN Representative, Sir Alexander Cadogan.[11] During 1948, the American official most active in dealing with Kashmir was Ambassador Klahr Huddle, who served as the US representative to UNCIP. Huddle found 'little to choose' between the Indian and Pakistani attitude. Huddle was put off both by what he regarded as Nehru's 'self-righteous intransigent stand' and by Pakistani Foreign Minister Zafrullah Khan's dealings with UNCIP which he found 'patronizing and approaching arrogance'.[12]

REACTION OF AMBASSADOR LOY HENDERSON

Loy Henderson, the American Ambassador in New Delhi from 1948 until 1951, was a blunt Cold Warrior, having developed a thorough dislike for the Soviet Union during service there in the 1920s. Moved from Soviet affairs in the State Department after US-Russian relations warmed, Henderson took charge of the Middle East Division. After he got in trouble again, this time from his opposition to America's pro-Israeli policies, the Truman administration sent Henderson off as the US Ambassador to India. In New Delhi, the envoy found Nehru's neutralism incompatible with his own hardline anti-Communist views. Their relationship was a testy one at best.

In preparing Washington for Nehru's first visit to the United States in the autumn of 1949, Henderson cautioned that the Prime Minister—'a vain sensitive emotional and complicated person'—considered the United States a 'land of crass commercialism' and 'undeveloped intellect' and appeared to share upper class English 'scorn for and distrust of things American'. At the same time, Henderson credited Nehru with a more positive side. He was, Henderson wrote, 'a man of warm heart, of genuine idealism, of shrewd discernment, and of considerable intellectual capacity. He is also an expert politician and a natural leader.'[13]

NEHRU VISITS AMERICA IN 1949: DEAN ACHESON'S IMPRESSIONS

Nehru's trip to America, which lasted three weeks, took the prime minister from coast to coast and gave him a chance to see much of the United States and to meet with a broad cross-section of its citizenry. In public, Nehru made an excellent impression as an eloquent advocate of India's fledgling democracy and as a spokesman for the newly independent nations of Asia. He was articulate in explaining his neutralist foreign policy to often skeptical American audiences who thought that India, as a democracy, should join with the United States and other democratic countries against the Communist bloc. Nehru expressed his hope for friendship but made it clear that India would not become a US political camp follower nor would he beg for economic aid.

Although the public accorded him a warm welcome and the liberal press praised him as the hope for free Asia following the fall of China to the Communists, US officials were less impressed.[14] Trying to establish a personal relationship with the Indian prime minister, Secretary of State Dean Acheson spent three hours in a private discussion at his home after a state dinner. 'But,' Acheson commented, 'he (Nehru) would not relax. He talked to me, as Queen Victoria said of

Mr Gladstone, as though I were a public meeting.' After their discussion roamed the globe, Acheson turned to South Asia. When he asked Nehru for a 'frank discussion of a practicable solution of the trouble over Kashmir. I (Acheson) got a curious combination of a public speech and flashes of anger and deep dislike of his opponents. . . . Both Nehru's ideas of procedure, which seemed to preclude negotiation, and his notions of the dispute itself made any possibility of settlement dim indeed.'[15]

Summing up his ambivalent feelings about the Indian leader, Acheson wrote:

> [Our talk] made a deep impression on me. I was convinced that Nehru and I were not to have a pleasant personal relationship. He was so important to India and India's survival so important to all of us, that if he did not exist—as Voltaire said of God—he would have to be invented. Nevertheless, he was one of the most difficult men with whom I have ever had to deal.[16]

NEHRU AND GEORGE McGHEE

George McGhee, the State Department official responsible for India as the Assistant Secretary for Near Eastern and South Asian Affairs from 1949 until 1951, had similarly less than flattering views about Nehru. McGhee first got to know the prime minister when he accompanied him during the US visit. He also met with the Indian leader in New Delhi during two trips to South Asia, the first in December 1949 and the second in March 1951. In his book, *Envoy to the Middle World,* McGhee wrote that Nehru had a 'chip on shoulder toward American high officials, who he appeared to believe could not possibly understand someone with his background'. According to McGhee, during Nehru's 1949 visit, he 'succeeded in making himself so unpopular with Americans generally that it would later prove difficult to muster support for helping meet India's urgent need for wheat'.[17] Indeed, two years later, it took the Truman administration, with McGhee in the lead role, some four months of hard slogging to get the US Congress to approve $190 million in order to send a badly needed 1 million tons of wheat to prevent possible famine in India.[18]

McGhee found Nehru fuzzy headed and not a clear thinker. After his December 1949 talk with the Indian leader, McGhee wrote that Nehru 'proceeded to ramble all over the lot in his own well-known form of double-talk. I kept waiting for something of substance that I would be able to report. There was nothing . . . it was a very unsatisfactory experience for me. . . . I was disappointed in his unwillingness to discuss important issues with me. I was pessimistic that we would ever be able to establish any real basis for understanding with Nehru.'[19]

McGhee's next encounter with the prime minister was in March 1951 at the height of the Korean war and when McGhee was trying to convince the US Congress to approve food aid for India. By then, conflicting American and Indian attitudes regarding the Korean conflict and the Cold War had hardened. When Nehru reiterated his well-known neutralist stance, McGhee felt privately that the Indian leader was 'hiding his head in the sand'. Still, even though McGhee was disappointed by Nehru's stance toward the Cold War, like his patron Dean Acheson he thought that Nehru and India were important for the world and deserved US support.[20] McGhee was less charitable about the Indian leader's position on Kashmir. The American aim, McGhee commented was 'to avert full-scale war between India and Pakistan—this was always a threat. Our efforts failed—because of Nehru'.[21]

CHESTER BOWLES: A NEHRU ADMIRER

Henderson's successor as US envoy in New Delhi was Chester Bowles, who after making a fortune in advertising in the 1920s and 1930s gained national prominence during the Second World War as the head of the Office of Price Administration (OPA), the czar of domestic price controls. Bowles entered politics in 1948 by winning election as governor of Connecticut and became an important figure in the liberal wing of the Democratic Party. After losing the 1950 elections, Bowles expressed interest in a diplomatic assignment and was delighted when President Truman asked him to go to India. Although a foreign policy novice, Bowles' outgoing style, his knack for people-to-people diplomacy and the close working relationship that he was able to establish with Prime Minister Nehru, proved a sharp contrast with his predecessor Loy Henderson. The latter, a career diplomat had little flair or interest in public diplomacy and was never able to establish more than a tense official relationship with Nehru. Unlike the dour and formal Henderson, Bowles captured the imagination of Indians by his informality and evident affection for their new country.

Indeed, in his memoirs, Bowles comes close to expressing hero worship for the Indian leader. Nehru, he wrote in *Ambassador's Report* published in 1954, not only won the hearts and minds of India's intellectual elite but that of the peasant masses as well. The former was not surprising given Nehru's elite pedigree, his English education, leadership role in the freedom struggle and his centre-left political philosophy and his skill as a communicator. That he also became the idol of the masses was harder to explain. Bowles felt that Gandhi having anointed Nehru as his successor and the dramatic 'legend of his life' as an aristocrat who struggled for India's freedom helped account for the public's enthusiasm for its Prime Minister.[22]

Bowles saw Nehru frequently and, like many other American liberals of that era, fell under his charm. 'He is the most articulate man I have ever heard in personal conversation', Bowles wrote. At the same time, Bowles recognized that Nehru had a closed mind with regard to Kashmir. 'On its [Kashmir's] beauty and history he had much to say, but on the present conflict with Pakistan, he was always reluctant to talk.'[23] More generally, and especially with regard to Communist China and Asia, Bowles accepted many of Nehru's views which corresponded with his own liberal and idealistic bent on foreign affairs.[24] In Washington, State Department officials praised Bowles' ability to sell the United States to India but were less charitable about the envoy's tendency to try to sell Indian views in the United States. Indeed, after returning to the United States in 1953, Bowles wrote the influential *Ambassador's Report* which urged greater American understanding for India's policies and much increased economic assistance to the fledgling democracy.

Bowles was clearly the odd man out among senior figures in the Truman administration in reaction to and appraisal of Jawaharlal Nehru. Although Bowles accepted the bona fides of India's neutralism, Truman, Acheson, McGhee and others in the foreign affairs hierarchy did not welcome Nehru's decision to chart a separate path for India, neither siding with the West nor with the Communist bloc. This was especially so in the aftermath of the Korean war in which 50,000 American soldiers gave their lives. At the same time, the Democrats respected the fact that Nehru appeared a committed democrat trying to institutionalize representative government in his country despite India's underdevelopment, poverty, illiteracy and caste and communal complexities and tensions.

The Eisenhower Administration (1953-1961)

The Republican administration that assumed power in Washington in January 1953, especially the new Secretary of State John Foster Dulles, had an even less positive view of India's leader. As far back as January

1947, Dulles, who at the time was a member of the US delegation to the United Nations, perceived pro-Communist tendencies in the Indian interim government. The cause for this view was his dealings with Nehru's foreign policy adviser, Krishna Menon. Dulles was only the first of many US officials whom Menon offended by his acerbic tongue and anti-American stance.

JOHN FOSTER DULLES AND NEHRU (1953)

Before becoming Secretary of State, Dulles had little direct knowledge of South Asia and had apparently read only two books about the region. One, *Life in India,* written by his grandfather, Rev. John Welsh Dulles, a Presbyterian missionary to India in the late nineteenth century, warmly praised British colonialism. The other was Jawaharlal Nehru's *Glimpses of World History* which the Indian leader had written from jail in the 1930s for his daughter Indira.[25] One can only wonder how Nehru's agnostic and pro-socialist views impressed the deeply religious and staunchly pro-free enterprise Dulles.

Shortly after assuming office, Dulles became the first Secretary of State to travel to India, undertaking a three week trip to the Middle East and South Asia in May 1953. His talks with Nehru left the American visitor unenthusiastic, to put it mildly. Dulles told the National Security Council after his return to Washington that while he was 'immensely impressed by the martial and religious qualities of the Pakistanis' (Dulles visited Karachi after his stop in New Delhi) and that he found Nehru 'an utterly impractical statesman'.[26] Their discussions in New Delhi ranged the globe with predictable differences, especially regarding the motives of the Communists and the war in Korea, then nearing its end.

On the problem of Kashmir, Nehru and Dulles, however, agreed that a plebiscite was not the best way to resolve the dispute and that dividing the state would be a better way. At the start of the Eisenhower administration, the State Department had concluded that partition of the state was 'the only solution that seems to have practical possibilities'.[27] Recalling the acrimonious and emotional votes in inter-War Europe, Dulles looked with disfavour on plebiscites. Not surprisingly, Nehru readily agreed. The secretary, however, backed off from pressing this approach in the face of the stiff opposition encountered in Karachi when he raised the idea.

On possible US arms assistance to Pakistan, Dulles can hardly have endeared himself to Nehru by the way he handled this sensitive issue.

When the question arose, the secretary stated that Washington had 'no present plans that would bring it into a military relationship with Pakistan that could reasonably be looked on as un-neutral regarding India'.[28] The trouble with Dulles' lawyer-like choice of the words was that for the Indians any US arms aid to Pakistan would be considered 'un-neutral'. This became amply clear in February 1954 when the decision to establish a military security relationship with the Pakistanis caused a furor in India.

VICE PRESIDENT NIXON DISLIKES NEHRU

Another senior figure in the administration who looked with disfavour on Nehru was Vice President Richard Nixon. As a Congressman and Senator from California, Nixon had staked out a strongly anti-Communist position on the conservative wing of the Republican Party. In December 1953, Eisenhower sent the young Vice President, then quite inexperienced in foreign affairs, on an extended goodwill trip to seventeen Asian countries, including India. The question of arms aid to Pakistan was being discussed intensively in Washington at that moment. Nixon, who described Nehru as 'the least friendly leader' whom he encountered in Asia, told journalists in Delhi, 'the U.S. should take a firmer course with Nehru who has often embarrassed the US'.[29]

The vice president made no bones about his support for giving military assistance with Pakistan in talking with newsmen during the trip or later when the National Security Council considered the issue.[30] In his 1982 book, *Leaders*, Nixon had the following mainly unflattering remarks about the Indian Prime Minister. 'Nehru,' Nixon wrote, 'would certainly rank among the most intelligent. He could also be arrogant, abrasive, and suffocatingly self-righteous, and he had a distinct superiority complex that he took few pains to conceal.'[31]

DULLES AND NEHRU MEET AGAIN (1956)

Although the US administration was well aware of Indian views, Dulles and his senior aide for the region, Assistant Secretary of State for the Near East and South Asia, Henry Byroade, underestimated the emotional intensity of India on the arms question. By the time Dulles visited New Delhi for the second time in early 1956, relations continued to remain strained. Disliked as the architect of the detested US-Pakistan alliance, Dulles had become so unpopular that he needed special police protection during the visit. An additional problem, which in fact was not of Dulles' making but due to an internal mixup in the State Department press office, was that the United States had voiced its support for the Portuguese position on Goa, which the Indians regarded as the last vestige of European imperialism in their territory.[32]

On most issues, the March 1956 Dulles-Nehru talks only confirmed the gap between the two leaders on major global issues. Nehru was optimistic about the prospect for early change within the Communist world in the wake of the blistering attacks by Nikita Khrushchev on Stalinism that the Soviet leader had made in the twentieth party congress in February 1956. Dulles agreed that there would be change but thought it would take at least a generation, far longer than Nehru anticipated.[33] Dulles proved far closer to the mark than the Indian prime minister. The fundamental change in Communism ushered in by Gorbachev occurred almost thirty-three years later in 1989.

Nehru also lashed out at Pakistan, speaking with much emotion in opposition to US arms aid. Pakistan, the Indian leader, charged (correctly as Pakistanis now freely admit) had entered the Western alliance system not to oppose the Soviets but 'to get strength against India'. Although Dulles reiterated the standard American position that arms given to Pakistan would not be used against India and denied that these were causing an arms race between the two countries, Nehru was not moved.[34] Had Nehru been able to read Dulles' mind, he would have been pleased by the extent that India's concerns about Pakistan had gotten through. In reporting on the talks, Dulles cabled Eisenhower, 'the one distinct impression that I gained is their almost pathological fear of Pakistan. I knew, of course, that they did not like our alliance with, and armament program for, Pakistan, but I never fully appreciated the full depth of their feeling.'[35] A better grasp on India's feelings about Pakistan did not, however, mean that the Secretary thought any better about Nehru's overall foreign policy. In a 9 June 1956 speech at Iowa State University, Dulles bared his teeth. 'Except under very exceptional circumstances', neutralism was, in Dulles' words, 'an immoral and shortsighted conception'.[36]

EISENHOWER: SOMEONE WHO LIKED NEHRU

President Eisenhower never fully shared Dulles' distaste for Nehru and was more sensitive than his secretary of state to the feelings of Asians. Unlike Dulles, Eisenhower had actually lived in the Far East and worked with Asians. For several years in the mid-1930s, he served as aide to General Douglas MacArthur, then Commander of the Philippine

Army. At that time, the Philippines were still an American colony but had begun the transition to full independence. 'India had also been a source of fascination', Eisenhower wrote in his memoirs. 'I had read about the modern development and government of India and frequently had expressed a hope of paying a visit to the subcontinent.' In 1949, when Eisenhower was serving as the President of Columbia University, he met Nehru and 'had been privileged to hold an extensive conversation with him'.[37]

After relations soured following the decision to arm Pakistan, Eisenhower, interested in improving ties with India, sent former Republican Senator John Sherman Cooper as Ambassador to Delhi in mid-1955. Eisenhower urged Cooper to try hard to establish a good personal relationship with Nehru, who the President felt was influenced as much 'by personality as by logical argument'. He also recommended that Dulles not make it harder for Cooper by asking him to do things that would impair his chances of developing rapport with the Indian leader.[38]

When Nehru visited the United States for a second time in December 1956, Eisenhower had just won re-election by an overwhelming majority. Having gained acclaim as free Asia's most prominent leader, Nehru was praised for having set India on the democratic path and for his determination to implement an ambitious development programme. India's success or failure in developing a free society was often seen as a contest with China's efforts to move ahead under Communism. Nonetheless, Nehru's waffling over the Soviet invasion of Hungary in November 1956 had tarnished his image. In contrast, Eisenhower's intervention to block the Anglo-French-Israeli attack on Egypt had boosted his standing, especially in the Third World.

Anxious to have relaxed talks with the Indian leader, Eisenhower arranged that Secretary Dulles would be away during much of the stay. Similarly Nehru made sure that Krishna Menon, who by then had become the *bête noire* for American officials, was not present. After receiving Menon in 1955 to discuss China, Eisenhower described the visitor in his diary as a 'menace and a boor'.[39] After greeting the Indian leader in Washington, the President took him off to his farm in nearby Gettysburg, Pennsylvania. The two spent a day and a half there alone and talked together for a total of fourteen hours in an informal setting.[40]

Substantively, their discussions, however, did not break new ground nor differ greatly from Dulles' talks in Delhi six months earlier. Nehru 'described his horrified reactions' to the Soviet repression of Hungary which he thought signaled the eventual deathknell of Communism. At the same time, the Prime Minister refused to agree that the Soviets were seeking world domination or posed a new form of colonialism. The leaders also disagreed in their appraisals of Communist China, but surprisingly seemed to agree that non-alignment was a wise course for India. Eisenhower was struck by Nehru's argument that given India's economic weakness, its becoming an ally would 'weaken not strengthen' the West. [41]

Eisenhower got an earful on Pakistan and Indian concerns about US arms assistance. Calling partition an 'egregious blunder', Nehru asserted that the people of Kashmir wanted to remain in India. In the memo Eisenhower dictated regarding the talks (some fourteen pages long), he admitted that Nehru did not have to justify his refusal to hold a plebiscite since he had forgotten to raise this question. When they discussed economic aid, the president was clearly listening. During a later cabinet discussion, Eisenhower showed much greater knowledge about Indian development plans than Treasury Secretary George Humphrey, a foe of foreign aid. The President even explained in a sympathetic way Indian plans to develop industries in the public sector.

Unlike Truman, Acheson and Dulles, Eisenhower liked Nehru even though he found him a person of 'unusual contradictions'. He credited the Indian leader with sincerely wanting 'to help his people and lead them to higher levels of living and opportunity'. At the same time, the American President remained puzzled by Nehru's 'tolerance relatively speaking of Soviet attitudes' even though he opposed their methods. Perceptively, Eisenhower thought this may have stemmed from resentment over Western 'condescension' towards India—a feeling the President thought that millions in Asia and Africa probably shared.[42] The 1956 Nehru-Eisenhower talks proved more than the usual exchange of views between heads of governments. Both leaders came away with greater sympathy and understanding of the other's positions.

A month later in his second inaugural address, Eisenhower reflected the growing US interest in the developing world, the showcase of which was India, and concern about the attractiveness of Communism to '[the] new forces and new nations [that] were stirring across the earth [seeking] freedom from grinding poverty'.[43] During Eisenhower's second term, the emphasis of US policy towards South Asia shifted from military assistance to economic aid and accordingly from Pakistan towards India.

An additional factor drawing the two countries closer was the mounting tension in the late 1950s between India and Communist China over their disputed borders in the Himalayas and the trouble between China and Tibet. When a May 1959 National Security Council meeting discussed using India as a counterweight against China, Eisenhower disagreed, noting India's reluctance to play such a role. In any case, echoing Nehru's comments, the President added that trying to make India a counterweight to China might bankrupt the United States. Eisenhower said that America's goal should be to 'give India a chance to grow as a free and democratic country,' adding, 'the Indians were wise to adopt their attitude of non-alignment'.[44] (One wonders what John Foster Dulles, who had by then died of cancer, would have thought of Eisenhower's comments.)

At the end of 1959, the President travelled to South Asia, using the new presidential Boeing 707, for the first time. It enabled the chief executive to travel far greater distances in increased comfort than the propeller driven aircraft Eisenhower had previously used. In fact, Eisenhower told a British visitor, Lord Plowden, that he planned the three week trip to Europe and the Middle East 'just to get to India'.[45] In his memoirs, Eisenhower underscored how Nehru in his 1956 visit had stirred the President's interest in India. 'I had become so intrigued by the picture he [Nehru] painted of the region, its people, and their aspirations that my desire to see that country for myself became the stronger.'[46]

On 10 December 1959, after two days in Karachi and a half-day in Kabul, the presidential jet landed in New Delhi near dusk. He was received with such enthusiastic crowds, the largest since India's Independence twelve years before, that the motorcade took over an hour to drive in from the airport. His four days in India included a visit to the Taj Mahal, an address to parliament and a speech to a vast crowd in front of the Red Fort. His extensive talks with Prime Minister Nehru touched on 'almost all the current problems of Asia, Europe and even Africa'. On China, Nehru expressed perplexity about the hardened position on the border dispute after he extended the hand of friendship to Beijing. In reviewing Indo-Pakistan difficulties, the President said he was 'perplexed' between his desire to provide military help to Pakistan (Eisenhower had been impressed with Pakistan's President General Mohammed Ayub Khan) and 'an equal wish not to cause embarrassment or anxiety to India'. Eisenhower insisted that the United States would never permit Pakistan to use US equipment to attack

India. Perhaps more to the point, he informed Nehru that Pakistan had only a limited capability since the United States provided only a week's supply of ammunition.[47]

Eisenhower wrote that he was enthralled by Nehru's description of 'India, her history, her principal problems, both domestic and foreign, and of his hopes for her' and found the Indian leader 'palpably honest and sincere'. Even though the President failed to bring India and Pakistan closer together during his visit, the trip was wildly successful. India showed that it liked Ike and Ike, in turn, clearly liked India. 'We were not out to get anything from each other', a positive Nehru wrote India's Chief Ministers, 'but rather to understand and I think both of us succeeded to some extent . . . I believe there is greater mutual understanding between these two countries now'.[48]

THE KENNEDY ADMINISTRATION (1961-1963)

In the 1960 presidential election, John F. Kennedy, the Democratic Party candidate, defeated his Republican foe, Vice President Nixon. Although South Asia did not loom large during the campaign, Kennedy had been critical of the Eisenhower administration's emphasis on military pacts with developing nations. As a senator from Massachusetts, he had also urged a substantial increase in economic aid for India in an October 1957 *Foreign Affairs* article and in a well-publicized 25 March 1958 speech in the Senate. In contrast to Nixon's negative appraisal of Nehru, Kennedy in his first State of the Union message on 30 January 1961 lauded the 'soaring idealism' of the Indian leader whom he praised as one of the great leaders of the twentieth century. Although put off by Nehru's preachy neutralism—in their first meeting, when Kennedy visited India in 1951, the Prime Minister showed little interest in the young Congressman—Kennedy still regarded India with its large population and democratic aspirations as the key developing nation and worthy of major attention from the United States.[49]

In November 1961, Nehru, then 71 years old, made what would be his last journey to the United States. Despite the fact that the Kennedy administration went all out to make the Indian leader's third official visit a success, it proved a disappointing failure. Kennedy's biographer, Arthur Schlesinger, quoted the President as describing the Nehru trip as 'the worst state visit I have had'.[50] According to India's Ambassador at the time, the capable B.K. Nehru, the problem was that the Prime

Minister was not only ageing but was in failing health.[51] Why the Kennedy administration was unaware of this is not entirely clear. Senior officials like NSC staffer Robert Komer and Assistant Secretary of State for the Near East and South Asia, Phillips Talbot blamed US Ambassador to India, John Kenneth Galbraith, the renowned Harvard economist, for failing to alert Washington about Nehru's physical condition and lack of energy.[52]

In an effort to get the visit off to a friendly and informal start, the President received Nehru at the Kennedy family residence in Cape Cod. When the 44-year old Chief Executive asked the veteran Asian leader for his views on the Vietnam problem, Nehru failed to give a coherent response and fell 'into remote silence'.[53] After they returned to Washington and met with advisors at the White House, Nehru remained similarly reticent. Kennedy did almost all the talking as he laid out US foreign policy goals and concerns. Nehru said little, leaving the President uneasy and puzzled. In a private session, Nehru unbent somewhat, but still remained passive in discussing the major issues of the day. He became animated only when he reviewed the Indian position on Kashmir. Kennedy had trouble keeping the conversation going and, according to Galbraith, later commented, 'it was like trying to grab something in your hand, only to have it turn out to be fog'.[54]

A morning session over coffee which Ambassador Nehru arranged at the Indian Embassy for the Prime Minister to meet with leading figures in the Kennedy administration turned out 'a disaster'. When Arthur Schlesinger asked about the role of intellectuals in India, Nehru talked in circles and failed to respond. He was similarly vague in answering other questions. Schlesinger commented, 'I had the impression of an old man, his energies depleted'.[55] Although none of his many close contacts in the Kennedy administration said so directly, Ambassador Nehru concluded that after the disappointing visit Kennedy 'wrote Nehru off as finished'.[56]

In fact, it was the humiliating defeat of Indian forces a year later during the October-November 1962 border conflict with China that effectively finished Nehru as a political leader. Even though he was ageing, he had remained in the public eye as Asia's leading international figure and the revered founding-father of India's democracy and the Non-Aligned Movement. The defeat by China with whom he had tried hard to develop friendship in the early 1950s was a staggering psychological blow from which he never recovered. As Galbraith wrote to Kennedy on 9 November 1962: 'One of the worst problems here is that the Chinese attack strikes the country with a very tired leader whose principles and ideas also have been badly shattered by the event.'[57] When a team led by W. Averell Harriman met with the Indian leader in late-November, 'Nehru looked tired and strained. It must have been difficult for him to greet Americans over the ruins of his long-pursued policy of neutralism', team member and senior U.S official Roger Hillsman wrote.[58]

POSTSCRIPT: 1964

In January 1964, Nehru suffered a debilitating stroke from which he never fully recovered. When Chester Bowles, who had returned to Delhi for a second ambassadorial assignment, and Assistant Secretary Talbot called on Nehru in March 1964, they were shocked by his condition. Nehru had difficulty in conversing coherently and hardly recognized the visitors.[59] On 27 May 1964, Jawaharlal Nehru died in his sleep.

Notes

1. G. Bhagat, *Americans in India, 1784-1860*, New York: New York University Press, 1970, pp. 3-84.
2. Harold Isaacs, *Scratches on Our Mind,* White Plains, NY: M.E. Sharpe, 1980, p. 265.
3. Ibid., p. 291.
4. Ibid., pp. 283-5.
5. Dennis Kux, *India and the United States, 1941-1991: Estranged Democracies*, Washington: National Defense University Press, 1993, pp. 23-4.
6. Johnson to Roosevelt, 11 April 1942. *Foreign Relations of the United States (FRUS), 1942,* vol. 1, Washington: Government Printing Office, 1960, pp. 631-2.
7. Gary Hess, *America Encounters India, 1941-1947*, Baltimore: Johns Hopkins University Press, pp. 166-7.
8. Harold Isaacs, *Scratches on Our Mind*, pp. 317-19.
9. Embassy, New Delhi, dispatch to State Department, 22 April 1947, 845.00/4-2247, State Department Records, National Archive, College Park, Maryland.
10. Embassy, Paris, to the State Department reporting Nehru-Marshall meeting, 20 October 1948. *FRUS, 1948*, vol. 5, p. 431.
11. Memorandum of conversation between Marshall and Cadogan, Paris, 10 November 1948. *FRUS, 1948,* vol. 5, pt. 1, pp. 445-8.
12. Embassy Karachi (Huddle) to the State Department, 15 July and 10 August 1948 and Embassy, Delhi (Huddle) to the State Department, 19, 21 and

27 July and 16 August 1948, *FRUS 1948*, vol. 5, pt. 1, pp. 349-53, 358, 362-5.

13. H.W. Brands, *Inside the Cold War: Loy Henderson and the Rise of the American Empire, 1918-1961*, New York: Oxford University Press, 1991, pp. 203-4.
14. Kux, *Estranged Democracies*, pp. 69-70.
15. Dean Acheson, *Present at the Creation*, New York: Norton & Co., 1969, pp. 335-6.
16. Ibid., p. 336.
17. George McGhee, *Envoy to the Middle World*, New York: Harper & Row, 1983, p. 47.
18. For fuller discussion of the wheat loan, see Kux, *Estranged Democracies*, pp. 79-82.
19. McGhee, *Envoy to the Middle World*, pp. 100-1.
20. Ibid., pp. 295-7.
21. Interview with George McGhee, Middleburg, Virginia, 14 August 1991.
22. Chester Bowles, *Ambassador's Report*, New York: Harper & Brothers, 1954, pp. 100-1.
23. Ibid.
24. Howard B. Schaffer, *Chester Bowles, New Dealer in the Cold War*, Cambridge, Mass.: Harvard University Press, 1993, p. 62.
25. Kurt Stiegler, 'John Foster Dulles and the 1954 United States-Pakistan Mutual Defense Agreement', Ph.D. diss., Texas A & M University, 1989, pp. 68-9.
26. Minutes of 1 June 1953 National Security Council meeting, *FRUS, 1952-1954*, vol. 9, pt. 2, p. 382.
27. Memoranda from Assistant Secretaries Byroade and Hickerson to Secretary Dulles, 14 March 1953 and from Dulles to President Eisenhower, 24 March 1953. Ibid., pp. 1314, 1316.
28. Dulles' report of his 22 May 1953 meeting with Nehru. Ibid., pp. 119-21.
29. *New York Times*, 9 and 10 December 1953.
30. Minutes of the 24 December 1953 National Security Council meeting, NSC series, Whitman File, Dwight D. Eisenhower Library, Abeline, Kansas. Selig Harrison, Associated Press correspondent in New Delhi in 1959, recalled the Nixon press conference which was on 'background' basis in a conversation with the author.
31. Richard M. Nixon, *Leaders*, New York: Warner Books, 1982, p. 271.
32. Dulles' press spokesman Carl McCardle explained in an oral history interview that the statement supporting the Portuguese was released in error and had not been fully vetted within the State Department. Once out, however, the damage was done. Carl McCardle Oral history, pp. 132-42, Dulles papers, Harvey Mudd Library, Princeton, New Jersey.
33. 14 March 1956. Jawaharlal Nehru, *Letters to Chief Ministers*, vol. 4, New Delhi: Jawaharlal Nehru Memorial Fund, 1988, p. 356.
34. Ibid., p. 351; Sarvepalli Gopal, *Jawaharlal Nehru: A Biography*, vol. 2: *1947-1956*, London: Jonathan Cape, 1979, p. 275; and memoranda of conversations

between Dulles and Nehru, 9-10 March 1956, *FRUS, 1955-1957*, vol. 8, pp. 306-8.

35. Telegram from Dulles to Eisenhower regarding the talks with Nehru, 11 March 1956. Ibid., pp. 309-11.
36. *New York Times*, 10 June 1956.
37. Eisenhower, *Waging Peace*, pp. 106-7.
38. Letter from Eisenhower to Dulles, 23 March 1955. *FRUS, 1955-1957*, vol. 8, p. 278.
39. Robert H. Ferrell (ed.), *The Eisenhower Diaries*, New York: W.W. Norton & Company, 1981, p. 300.
40. Eisenhower, *Waging Peace*, p. 108.
41. Ibid., pp. 109-10, 112-13. Sarvepalli Gopal, *Jawaharlal Nehru: A Biography*, vol. 3: *1956-1964*, London: Jonathan Cape, 1984, p. 41.
42. Eisenhower, *Waging Peace*, pp. 113-14.
43. Stephen E. Ambrose, *Eisenhower: The President*, New York: Simon & Schuster, 1984, pp. 377-81.
44. Record of the 28 May 1959 National Security Council meeting. *FRUS, 1958-1960*, vol. 15, p. 9.
45. Memorandum of conversation with Lord Plowden, Chairman of the UK Atomic Energy Commission, 13 November 1959. Ibid., p. 521.
46. Eisenhower, *Waging Peace*, p. 487.
47. Sarvepalli Gopal, *Jawaharlal Nehru: A Biography*, vol. 3, p. 104; Memorandum of conversation between Eisenhower and Nehru, 10 December 1959, *FRUS, 1958-1960*, vol. 15, pp. 521-4.
48. 15 December 1959. Jawaharlal Nehru, *Letters to Chief Ministers*, vol. 5: *1958-1964*, New Delhi: Jawaharlal Nehru Memorial Fund, 1989, p. 343.
49. Arthur M. Schlesinger, Jr., *A Thousand Days: John F. Kennedy in the White House*, Boston: Houghton Miflin Company, 1965, p. 522.
50. Ibid., p. 526.
51. Interview with B.K. Nehru, 12 January 1991, New Delhi.
52. Interviews with Robert Komer, 5 August 1990, Washington, and Phillips Talbot, 26 June 1990, New York.
53. Schlesinger, Jr., *A Thousand Days*, p. 524 and B.K. Nehru interview.
54. Ibid.
55. Schlesinger, Jr., *A Thousand Days*, p. 525 and B.K. Nehru interview.
56. Ibid.
57. Letter from Galbraith to Kennedy, 9 November 1962, John F. Kennedy Library, Boston, Massachusetts.
58. Memorandum for the record on meeting with Nehru, 25 November 1962 drafted by Roger Hilsman, State Department director of intelligence and research, JFK Library.
59. Interview with Phillips Talbot, 26 June 1990, New York.

SERGEY LOUNEV

❖ The Soviet Perception of India's Foreign Policy in the 1940s-1950s

Soviet policy towards India has been attracting attention of a number of Soviet, Indian and Western scholars since a 'special relationship' was established between the leader of the former socialist camp and military superpower and the 'world largest democracy', a powerful developing country and an informal leader of the Non-Aligned Movement. There were many reasons, both scholarly and practical, for a profound interest in Soviet-Indian relations. The Indian anchor has played a very special role in the Soviet Third World strategy as well as in the Soviet global strategy. It has greatly enhanced the flexibility of the ideological foundations of the Soviet foreign policy and has influenced the configuration of forces in South and South-East Asia. Soviet involvement in the affairs of the subcontinent also served as a point of reference for important questions such as international conflict management/ reduction, North-South trade regulation, superpower confrontation on regional issues and relationship between a superpower and a regional power, etc.

There exists a rather solid body of Western literature on this subject, and some of the books have already became classics such as works by William Barnds, Robert Donaldson, Robert Hardgrave. Monographs by Arthur Stein, Robert Horn, Stanley Wolpert, Timothy George, Shahram Chubin and Robert Litvak are worthy of mention as well.[1] Quite a lot has been written in India, probably much more than in the West.[2] At the same time, it seems, there is still a certain gap in the literature. What is lacking is an analysis making the case that India was an integral part of Soviet foreign policy and strategy in the developing world. This question forms part of a bigger theme: what were Soviet national interests (or perceived as national by the former Soviet leadership)? Other shortcomings in the study of this theme can be attributed to the shortage of information on the problem, owing to the difficulty of understanding highly ideologized and sometimes irrational former Soviet-Indian politics.

Soviet scholars have not presented a comprehensive study of the field either. Moreover, during Soviet times, there was not a single monograph published on the problems of Soviet-Indian relations. One may mention only dispensable articles regularly published in commemoration of different anniversaries and official visits. Sometimes Soviet scholars published their works abroad.[3] But they had to be very cautious because of political considerations. It is true that during the Soviet era, scholars could not discuss openly any important questions of foreign policy. It was a field completely closed for criticism, and their task was usually limited to approving and substantiating the political course of the Soviet leadership. Since then the situation has not improved greatly, Russian scholars now have absolute freedom of discussion but have lost interest in Soviet foreign policy. In the 1990s, only one book was published on the theme but it is rather a journalistic work than an academic one.[4]

Indian scholarly literature has always been more open, but naturally it presented an Indian perspective on the events that may often be different from a Soviet viewpoint. Besides some delicate issues like collision of Soviet and Indian interests were also usually bypassed. Hence, the scrutinizing of the Soviet diplomatic archives gives an opportunity not only to analyse the main axes of the Indian foreign policy from the point of view of the Soviet diplomacy but to fill in some gaps in the study of Soviet-Indian relations as well.

These relations had an asymmetric character. The changes were mainly linked with the momentous shifts in: (a) the global system of international relations, and (b) the internal development of the Soviet Union that had affected the external dimension of Soviet para-strategy. Principally, six stages of bilateral relations can be discerned: (1) 1947-56; (2) 1956-71; (3) 1971-9; (4) 1979-85; (5) 1985-8; (6) 1988-91. After the collapse of the Soviet Union and, with it, the disappearance of a superpower, it is possible to discuss the equality of standing in the international community of India and Russia. If the current socio-economic tendencies remain in the future, the bilateral relations will again have an asymmetric character, but now India will be a leading partner.[5]

Historical Overview: Soviet Interests in India

Though historically there existed certain cultural and commercial ties between Russia and India, they were very limited and there is really no grounds to argue that Russia and India have any common past and are linked by traditional ties (of course there existed very close ties between Central Asia and India, but they hardly ever seriously influenced the 'central' Russian policy or the perceptions of India in Russia). Even when in the nineteenth century Russia started its advance in Asia for different reasons (partly because of British policy, Russia never established a serious direct contact with India), its main objective, however remote, was to squeeze out Great Britain' role in the region and to spread Russian influence at least to northern India. In 1801, Russian Czar Pavel I sent Cossacks, via Hiva, to India. These plans were stopped by the *coup d'état* in which Ch. Witwort, Britain's Ambassador to Russia, took an active part and during which the Emperor was killed. After conquering Central Asia in 1885, India grew in importance in the eyes of the Russian Empire (Russia even tried to intervene in a *coup d'état* in Nepal on the side of one of the contenders), but it was essentially left to the Russian intelligence service to signify this interest. It should also be noted that during this period, studies on India reached a peak in Russia.

After the Bolshevik Revolution, the new leaders of the Soviet Union turned their attention to the Afro-Asian world. The leaders of the revolution did not expect a rapid triumph of socialism in Russia which they viewed as sort of an ignition cord that should be burned up completely for the sake of the revolutionary renovation of the world. The 'World Revolution' ranked highly among the main slogans of the October Revolution. But the hopes for European proletarian uprising definitely faded by the 1920s. The Hungarian Soviet Republic and the Bavarian Soviet Republic had been utterly defeated, the Soviet republics in the Baltic region and in Finland had fallen. The last illusions about European proletariat perished in the course of the Soviet-Polish war of 1920 when the majority of the Polish population was driven not by 'class interests', but rather by their national sentiments.

From there came the interest of the Soviet leaders to the Orient and the idea that close ties between revolutionary Russia and Afro-Asian nations may lead in a roundabout way to the victory of the new system on a worldwide scale. In 1921, Lenin said that the outcome of the struggle for liberation would be determined by the fact that Russia, India and China made the majority of the world's population and they had been rapidly induced in the struggle for their own liberation. In that sense, he added, there could not be even a shadow of a doubt what would be the final outcome of the world struggle—a full and final victory of socialism was guaranteed.[6] As early as in 1920, Stalin wrote that the liberation of India would strengthen the position of socialism in the whole world.[7] Evidently he expected India to join the socialist camp.

After the October Revolution, Russia presented itself as an example to some Indian nationalists. Marxist circles were founded in India and Jawaharlal Nehru visited Moscow in 1927. But though the Indian Communists took part in the Communist International and in a sense obeyed its decisions, they never presented any serious political challenge either to the British or to the main Indian national parties—the Indian National Congress and the Muslim League. Neither did Nehru become a communist neophyte after his visit to Moscow. Though he was really impressed by the rapid economic development of the Soviet Union under a centralized planning system (and later accepted this principle with serious modifications as a cornerstone of his economic policy when he became the first Prime Minister of India) and fostered certain socialist ideas, he never was a Moscow ideological ally.

In the Orient at this time only China justified the hopes of the Soviet leaders. Since the middle of the 1920s, the appeals to export revolution disappeared and the attitude of Stalin's regime towards India became cold. Until the end of the 1940s, there was no particular Soviet interest in India and the only channel for any Soviet involvement in India was through the Indian Communists. But this channel proved to be a dead end for any serious success because Stalin's ideological dogmas that were compulsory to all communist parties in Asia precluded any cooperation with what was called the 'national bourgeoisie', the only real power in India.

The outcome of the Second World War, the so-called 'people's revolutions' in Eastern Europe and China, once again allowed the Soviet leadership to consider the possibility to establish a 'worldwide republic of Soviets'. The attitude of India was extremely disillusioning for Stalin's regime because it did not fit into a bipolar representation of the world (it is fair to say the same about the Truman's administration) where 'who is not with us, is against us'.

Soviet-Indian Relations in 1946-1949

Besides ideological impediments to any Soviet involvement in India, there existed other, more tangible reasons. During these post-War years, when American-British forces began the Cold War against the USSR, the Soviet Union did not direct any resources for an active policy in South Asia. All resources were directed to the reconstruction and to the development of an atomic and nuclear potential that was indispensable for the confrontation with the West and its survival (the US had developed plans of nuclear bombardment of all the largest cities of the USSR). The Soviet Union, moreover, did not have any special interest in South Asia. Its primary effort was directed to the European battlefield where the Soviet Union was busy establishing and strengthening its East European empire. In the Orient, which was far less important, Soviet interests were supposedly taken care of by the Red Revolution in China.

What was later labelled as 'the Third World' was of no special interest to Moscow as it was located too far from the main Soviet adversaries to make it a valuable asset in its struggle against them. Furthermore, it did not present any special economic opportunity as the Soviet Union itself had potential resources in plenty, but was short of investments and had neither transport nor naval capability of developing and protecting its own global trade. At that time full mutual deterrence, that later made a strategic nuclear war unacceptable to the two power blocs and compelled them to substitute it by fighting each other in remote regions, often by proxy, was not achieved.

At the same time, the Soviet Union was firmly supporting the national liberation movements in the East and so too did the United States. Both powers were striving to establish their superpower status. But the former pre-war world system with colonial powers and colonies, prevented them from achieving greater successes (the colonial power was able to restrict any attempt by any other power to develop ties with its colonies). In view of this, the Soviet leadership understood that India played a special role. The Deputy Minister of Foreign Affairs of the USSR, Jakov Malik, wrote to the Soviet Foreign Minister, Vyacheslav Molotov, in a secret letter dated 27 February 1947, that it was necessary to establish diplomatic relations with India as soon as possible, 'taking in consideration both the peculiarities and special features of India's international role and her position in Asia and in the system of colonial countries'.[8]

All these considerations underlined the first stage of Soviet-Indian relations. Even before India achieved Independence, the purposes and principles of its foreign policy had been worked out by the Indian National Congress, thanks mainly to Nehru who had been moulding it since the early 1930s. The principles included battling imperialism and colonialism, granting equal rights for all races, upholding the essential part of Asian and African countries in world politics, sustaining peace all over the world, striving to allay the strain in international situation and achieving general disarmament, abstaining from the use of force to settle disputes, ensuring true independence in the sphere of foreign policy, and promoting friendly relations with all countries. As early as in September 1946, in his first seminal speech on India's foreign policy, Nehru conveyed to the world that India would stay away the power blocs. Few days later, on 21 September, Nehru sent a letter to the Soviet Foreign Minister, Molotov, wherein he wrote, 'Krishna Menon is sent by me on a mission as my personal representative. We sincerely want to develop friendly relations with the USSR and exchange diplomatic and other representatives.'[9] Molotov agreed completely with that suggestion but, in view of the drought in the Soviet Union, he refused to supply food grains to India which Nehru had requested for.[10] On 31 October 1946, V.K. Krishna Menon met Molotov in New York. The Soviet Foreign Minister suggested to him to come to Moscow for negotiations with the Deputy Minister of Foreign Affairs of the USSR, but Krishna Menon explained that he preferred to discuss the problems with Molotov personally. The next round of negotiations was held in February 1947 in London.[11] Jakov Malik wrote that 'Nehru is interested in the establishment of diplomatic relations with the USSR due to both internal and external considerations'[12] but 'the Hindus are under direct pressure of Englishmen or have apprehensions of them'.[13] Indeed, the declassified India Office archives show that the British Foreign Office did everything possible to prevent the establishment of Soviet-Indian diplomatic relations. Their intrigues failed only due to the firm position of Nehru[14] and on 13 April 1947 Moscow and Delhi declared the establishment of diplomatic relations. The Soviet leaders could not but notice India's desire to be neutral. As early as 1946, a certain similarity in the viewpoints of the interim government and the USSR on a number of international problems could be seen. This was more than evident all through the 1946 session of the UN General Assembly and greatly worried the United States.[15]

On 15 August 1947, the first government of independent India headed by Nehru endeavoured to sustain the principles of foreign policy outlined by the Indian National Congress before Independence. The government of India managed to give real content to the foreign policy shaped in the 1930s. Principles formulated during the Congress session at Jaipur in 1948 became India's official position. The philosophical convictions of Indian leaders, such as Nehru, singularly orchestrated the practical conduct of Indian foreign policy. At that stage, India strove mainly to avoid being drawn into a probable new world war, to achieve real independence in the sphere of foreign policy, and to expand its foreign trade and obtain greater help from other countries to develop its economy. India could realize these aims only if it refrained from joining the military conflict of states belonging to either of the two world systems. Such principles and aims were in consonance with the endeavour of India's ruling élite to ensure the country's political independence and achieve economic independence as well. The process was sustained by the anti-imperialist traditions of the national liberation movement and the mass struggle for consolidating independence and accomplishing social progress.

The messages from the Soviet Embassy in Delhi constantly stressed that disagreement between the US and India in solving vital international problems was growing. This was evident from the UN discussions of problems such as racism and colonialism. For example, in 1946-8, Indian and American viewpoints on apartheid in South Africa were constantly at variance as the Indian government and the Indian public opinion vehemently opposed the South African racist regime. The position of India and the USSR on the colonial war waged by the Netherlands against Indonesia (1947-9) also coincided.

But the Soviet leaders still remained reluctant in considering India as a fully neutral country. A typical Soviet statement was, 'the thesis that India should not have to do both with the US and the Soviet Union in order to keep the neutrality in the Third World War, allegedly unavoidable between two blocs . . . is used in practice to justify the policy of cooperation with England'.[16] Indeed, throughout that period, India's relations with capitalist countries, Great Britain in particular, remained rather close. The former metropolis' economic and political impact continued unabated. In 1949, it was proclaimed that India meant to stay within the Commonwealth. Some members of the Indian ruling circle had great hopes that the United States would offer economic assistance. In March 1949, Nehru remarked, 'When I say that we should not align ourselves with any power blocks, obviously it does not mean that we should not be closer in our relations with some countries than with others. That depends on entirely different factors, chiefly economic, political, and many other factors. At the present moment you will see that as a matter of fact we have far closer relations with some countries of the Western world than with others.'[17] Indeed, an analysis of India's voting pattern in the UN during the fifth session of the General Assembly shows that on 38 occasions India's vote mirrored that of the US while opposing Washington only twice.

Nor were the Soviet leaders very sympathetic to India's efforts at becoming the leader of Asia. USSR participation in the Asian Relations Conference (Delhi, March-April 1947) proceeded from the consideration of a 'zero-sum game'. The Head of the Department of South-East Asia wrote to Molotov, 'the attitude of Englishmen to the organisation of the international conference is obviously negative'. The aims of India were seen as following; (1) to unite Asian countries for the struggle against colonial policies in Asia, first of all, against English imperialism; (2) to turn India into the leading Asian country and to enhance by that the international prestige of India; (3) to avoid the restrictions put on foreign policy of India by the English government; and (4) to strengthen the internal and external positions of the Indian interim government.'[18]

The result of the conference was less positive. The report of the Main Political Department (GPU) of the armed forces of the USSR asserted that many speeches 'were badly camouflaged appeals for the unification of the Asian peoples against European ones and resembled the notorious theories of Japanese imperialists about 'Pan-Asian unity'.[19] The report of the head of the Soviet delegation to the ARC (28 April 1947) stated that the aim of the conference had been to 'create a permanent institute of international relations in order to turn India step by step into the ideological centre of a Pan-Asian bloc' and that the 'Indian big bourgeoisie is soliciting for taking over Japan's place in Asian markets'.[20] India's aspirations of strengthening its authority over the developing countries was not acceptable to the Soviet leadership.

Soviet-Indian relations were strained and it was due primarily to the USSR's mistrust of Indian leaders. The part played by the Indian bourgeoisie in the country's progress towards self-determination after gaining independence was misunderstood by the Soviet Union and it had negative consequences. The rightist circles, who supposedly instigated Nehru to tilt the country in favour of the West, were considered to be 'fascists and ultra-reactionaries' not only in secret documents of the Foreign Ministry and the Committee of the CPSU, but also in the media. The attitude towards the so-called 'big capitalists' in the leadership of the INC (Vallabhbhai Patel, Purushottamdas Tandon, etc.) was also very negative. The Soviet leaders had also a distaste for Mahatma Gandhi. So, in the aforementioned report on the ARC, the head of the Soviet delegation wrote with extreme disgust that the first

Indian Ambassador to the USSR, Vijayalakshmi Pandit, Nehru's own sister, was seen publicly kissing Mahatma Gandhi's feet.[21] Possibly the answer to the rather irrational attitude of the Soviet leaders can be found in the same report: 'Krishna Menon suggested to organise our meeting with Gandhi . . . but we refused as the progressive part of the Indian society has a very negative attitude vis-à-vis Gandhi.'[22]

'The progressive part' was an euphemism for the Communists in official Russian language. Evidently the Communists considered Gandhi to be their main rival in the struggle for the souls of ordinary Indians. Before the establishment of diplomatic relations, Soviet leaders received practically all the information about India through the Indian Communists. After the October Revolution, the leadership of Russia lost all other sources of information. British colonial authorities made sure that any Soviet citizen would be refused admittance to India. Even the intelligence network in India was lost as Bolsheviks had severed all such ties. It is no coincidence that in one of his first messages to Molotov (11 November 1947), the first Soviet Ambassador to India, K.V. Novikov, acknowledged that Moscow had no specialists on India, no knowledge of the situation in India and determined that the primary aims of the Embassy were the study of: (a) economic and social conditions in India; (b) internal policy; (c) foreign policy; (d) military-strategic situation; and (e) the political parties. The only other, 'non-academic', goal of the Embassy was prescribed as 'the establishment of cultural ties and the conduct of propaganda regarding the Soviet achievements'.[23] However, some acquaintance with Indian realities did help the Soviet Ambassador after the assassination of Gandhi. Even though Stalin refused to send his condolences, Novikov passed on the condolences to Nehru in the name of the Soviet government. Subsequently, the Soviet Foreign Ministry did send official condolences.[24]

During that period, the attitude of the Soviet leaders towards the Indian Prime Minister was very cautious and rather cold. He was considered to be a 'controversial figure'. On the one hand, fingers were pointed to 'Nehru's recent caution towards the US'[25], and on the other, Soviet officials suspected that the Indian leader was not really interested in developing friendly relations with the USSR. For example, the report on the Asian Relations Conference asserted that Nehru was interested in having India benefiting from the Soviet achievements; but also, that he 'had specially digressed from talks about political problems' during the meeting with the Soviet delegation ('Nehru's daughter [Indira Gandhi] began speaking with us about Moscow and he made her leave the meeting immediately') and he had tried to persuade it not to travel around India.[26]

It is necessary to point out that the attitude of senior Soviet officials was milder than the one adopted by the leadership. In the 1940s, the first draft of the annual telegrams of congratulations sent by J. Stalin to J. L. Nehru was much more friendly than the final version. For example, on the Prirne Minister's anniversary, the first draft had the words 'friendly congratulations', but the telegram eventually sent to Nehru on 13 November 1948, contained only 'best regards'.[27] The first draft of the telegram that Stalin sent to Nehru for the first Independence Day celebration had the words 'best regards to you personally and to the Indian people' while the telegram sent on 15 August 1948 contained only 'the wishes of best successes to the Indian people'. The following year, a similar telegram had the words 'my wishes of well-being to the Indian people'.[28] It was in stark contrast to the messages of Nehru to Stalin where the Indian Prime Minister wrote, for example, 'cordial and best wishes'.[29] Sometimes Nehru was obviously irritated by the cold tone of the Soviet leader. In his message dated 13 July 1950, the Indian Prime Minister wrote 'with the highest respect'. On receiving Stalin's reply (15 July 1950) containing the words 'with respect', Nehru used the same words in his next letter (16 July 1950).[30]

Moscow had certain apprehensions about the left-wing of the INC. The Soviet leaders considered, quite naturally all persons who had fought against Germany or its allies to be friends of the USSR (that is why in 1942 the Indian Communists did not participate in the Quit India movement as Britain was an ally of the Soviet Union). In this regard, the activities of Subhas Chandra Bose during the Second World War could not attract much sympathy, yet the recent speculations in India about the alleged imprisonment of Bose in the Soviet Union after the war are baseless. There is not one such evidence in the Soviet diplomatic archives.

The internal situation in India was the main reason for the indifferent bilateral relations. Left forces that demanded severing of ties with the former metropolis, with the United States and with the West in general, agitated violently against the government towards the end of the 1940s. Repression against Communists and sister organizations was conducted on a large scale. Moreover, the Soviet representatives in India were the constant object of harassment and intimidation. In 1948, Indian police encroached upon the territory of the Soviet

Embassy. The Soviet literature was often banned. In a message to Stalin sent on 22 September 1951, the Soviet Foreign Minister, A.Y. Vyshinsky, and the Minister for Foreign Trade, M.A. Men'shikov, recommended not to accept Novikov's proposal of opening a special theatre for the screening of Soviet films in Bombay. They asserted that 'only few films from the Soviet Union and other people democracies were allowed by the Indian censorship to be shown'.[31] Indeed, in 1948, for example, Bombay authorities forbade any screening of Soviet films. The diplomatic archives are full of accounts of attacks against the cinema halls where the Soviet films were shown. Furthermore, visas were often denied to different Soviet delegations.

The foreign policy of the Indian government was handicapped by domestic pressure. The Congress party right-wing was very powerful. 'Indian monopolist capital' (the term used by Soviet officialdom) was interested in widening contacts with the United States, primarily in the economic sphere. Indian right-wing parties criticized the government for improving relations with socialist countries and constantly called for cementing ties with the West. And there were the Indian elite's traditional relations with Great Britain. Centrist and right-wing circles had had a long-standing experience of British political culture, whether liberal-democratic or conservative-liberal. Many Indian officials were British by origin or had accepted the traditional British norms. They had great mistrust of the USSR and the Soviet citizens. That is why there was no real progress, even in such sub-systems as bilateral relations in cultural or economic spheres. In 1947-9, only barter trade agreements were concluded. In 1949, the Soviet Ambassador began negotiations on a joint trade treaty. According to Soviet sources, the Indian side was to be blamed for the delay in finalizing the treaty.[32]

All attempts by the first Indian Ambassador to the USSR, Vijayalakshmi Pandit (1947-9), to develop cultural ties between the two countries failed. She tried several times to get permission to publish a magazine about Indian culture (in Russian) and to send Indian students to the Soviet Union, but the Soviet leaders turned down these requests.[33] Even personal letters written by Nehru to the USSR Academy of Sciences inviting prominent scientists to India evoked no positive response (Nehru did not write rightly the name of the organization but his choice of personalities for a small team of scientists on a short visit was excellent. He had selected half of the future Nobel laureates from the Soviet Union).[34]

Soviet-Indian Relations in 1950-1952

At the beginning of the 1950s, Soviet-Indian relations showed signs of improvement because of some changes in Indian foreign policy and the refusal of Delhi to toe the American line. After the creation of the People's Republic of China (PRC) in 1949, the American administration feared the sweeping consolidation of relations between the USSR and the PRC as it posed a threat to its own positions in Asia. Hence, in great haste it started to look for someone to counterbalance China in Asia and hoped India might prove useful in that respect. Nehru's first visit to the US (October-November 1949) took place under these circumstances. The objectives of his visit was to obtain support on Kashmir and reach an agreement as regards economic assistance to India. The US administration intended drawing India into the policy of 'containment of communism' in Asia and into a political and military alliance with the Western states. None of the tasks were achieved. Nehru stated quite clearly that India was not going to change its neutralist course of foreign policy in return for American economic aid. The American administration in turn refused to grant India 1 million tons of wheat that it asked for and to supply technical assistance. A month after the visit, India announced its recognition of the PRC. The decision was based on a judicious analysis of the situation as there was a new and mighty neighbour appearing on India's frontiers. Added to this was the prospect of having trade relations with PRC. The United States was quite displeased with India's action and did not hide its disapproval. Of course, the Soviet leaders were highly satisfied with Indian position. Moscow watched very attentively the serious disagreement arising between India and the US on such international issues as the Korean war, the admission of the PRC to the UN and the conclusion of a peace treaty with Japan.

In June 1950 the Korean war began and the Indian government first voted for the UN resolution declaring North Korea to be the aggressor and calling upon UN members to supply assistance to South Korea.[35] But there were other factors operating meanwhile: India's fear of a full-fledged war between the East and the West, its wish to maintain its neutral course, and its attempts not to arouse suspicion of having joined the Western bloc. Further, New Delhi refused to send its forces to join the UN troops. Instead it sent to Korea only a medical service detachment. The Indian government had hopes of playing the mediator's role too. A week after the war in Korea began, B.N. Rao, India's representative in Korea, tried to arrange a consultation between the representatives of the USSR and the US. On 1 July 1950, Indian Ambassador to Russia, Sarvepalli Radhakrishnan, met Deputy Minister of Foreign Affairs of the USSR, V.A. Zorin, and suggested the setting up of a tripartite commission consisting of the USSR, the US and India to replace the Korean Commission of the UN. In his 3 July 1950 message to Stalin, First Deputy Minister of Foreign Affairs of the USSR, Andrei A. Gromyko, refused the offer because, to the USSR, 'foreign interference into the internal affairs of Korea [was] intolerable'.[36]

On 9 July 1950, the Indian Ambassador to the USSR sent a message to Gromyko to enquire about the attitude of the Soviet government towards the following suggestions: '(1) the US supports the admission of the PRC to the UN; (2) the Security Council—with the USSR[37] and the PRC—supports the immediate cessation of hostilities in Korea, the withdrawal of North Korean troops to the 38th parallel, after which the process of reunification of independent Korea begins through the mediation of the UN.'[38] Gromyko answered (the text had been approved by the Central Committee of the Communist Party) that the Soviet Union supported in principle the peaceful settlement of the Korean problem and that all the concrete questions should be considered by the Security Council or its permanent members — 'with indispensable participation of a representative of People's China'.[39] On 13 July 1950, Nehru sent personal letters to Stalin, the Chairman of the Soviet of Ministers of the USSR, and to Dean Acheson, the US Secretary of State, suggesting that the conflict be localized and that peaceful resolution of the Korean problem ought to be achieved quickly.[40] In his message to Stalin, the Indian Prime Minister wrote, 'I dare address a personal appeal to you to use your high authority and ascendancy for the achievement of this joint goal. The happiness of the mankind depends on it.'[41] In his reply of 15 July Stalin 'greeted the peaceful initiative'[42] and on 16 July, Nehru announced that he would immediately contact all the interested parties. The Indian Prime Minister shared with Moscow all his communications with Acheson.[43]

The insistence of Nehru on the PRC being admitted to UN, in opposition to the US position, was one of the reasons for the US refusing the Indian suggestion of finding a peaceful solution to the Korean problem. All Indian efforts naturally failed. The crossing of the 38th parallel by the American army under UN's ensign, the American air forces bombing of civil constructions and Truman's threat of using the atomic bomb, forced the Indian government to condemn certain aspects of the American policy. In the UN debates, India refused assent to the resolution permitting the UN forces to cross the 38th parallel (October 1950) and the one, in January 1951, which proclaimed the PRC to be the aggressor in Korea. Moscow reacted quite positively to these shifts, though the Soviet leaders complained about India's 'inconsistency'. In their talks with the Soviet leaders, the Indian diplomats began criticizing openly the US policy in the Far East. On 22 March 1952, Ambassador Radhakrishnan told Soviet Foreign Minister, Vyshinsky, that 'American Pentagon should be blamed for all things, but the peoples of the West are not going to be involved in the aggression on American order. . . . India has always supported the USSR on the political problems of the Far East.'[44]

In the early 1950s, the similarity of the stand of India and the Soviet Union (and the differences with the US) became more and more pronounced. In September 1951, India refused to sign the San Francisco treaty with Japan because the treaty proposed that the Ryukyu and Bonin Islands should be placed in the custody of the US and that the American military forces should stay in Japan. The Indian government wanted the treaty to include items such as the restoration of Taiwan to the PRC in future and the formal accession of the Kurile Islands and the Southern Sakhalin to the Soviet Union. India also opposed other US actions, such as its active support of France in its colonial war against the peoples of Indo-China, or even refusing to have the Tunisian problem considered by the UN Security Council in 1952 when a group of Afro-Asian countries brought the problem to the attention of the seventh session of the UN General Assembly.

The neutralist course of Indian foreign policy, notwithstanding its frequent vacillations, irritated Washington that looked at the world through the prism of 'bipolarity' and sought for new possible allies and new military bases in Asia. India was still much closer to the West, its representatives in the UN more often than not voted with the US and against the USSR. But it was the Soviet Union that began supporting India actively as a participant in the proposed political conference on Korea, whereas the US did its best not to admit India. The result was that India could not obtain the required number of votes to push the resolution through (though the USSR and other socialist countries voted for it).

The attitude of the Soviet leaders towards India softened. Moscow was pleased that after the death of the Deputy Prime Minister, Vallabhbhai Patel, in December 1950, and P. Tandon's having to leave the post of President of the Congress party, the positions of the right-wing inside the Congress were weakened. In 1951, for the first time, a telegram from Stalin congratulating Nehru for the Republic Day contained the words 'best regards to you personally and to the Indian people' (as was suggested in the first draft).[45] Stalin received S. Radhakrishnan twice (in January 1950 and April 1952). It was unusual for the Chairman of the Soviet of Ministers of the USSR to receive ambassadors. Stalin received foreign ambassadors very rarely and never received anyone twice. Moreover, he was greatly impressed by the personality of Indian Ambassador. [46] In 1952, the Soviet representative to the UN, Jakov Malik, supported India on the Kashmir problem so vehemently that Nehru was surprised and had to explain to the US and Great Britain that he had not asked the USSR for its support.[47]

The attitude towards Nehru was still contradictory. All the papers of the Russian diplomatic archives concerning the proposed visit of the Indian Prime Minister to Moscow are alike. They contained a slightly different version of the postponements of the visit from the one proposed by a number of authors: it was only Moscow to be blamed. According to Russian sources, on 16 December 1946 Krishna Menon proposed Nehru's visit to Moscow during a meeting with Novikov. Soviet officials advised the suitability of the visit after the establishment of diplomatic relations. On 8 August 1947, Ambassador Pandit repeated to Vyshinsky the desire of her brother to come to Moscow in 1947. On 3 January 1948, the Indian Ambassador told Molotov that 'this spring Nehru hopes to visit the Soviet Union' and the reply was, 'it would be good'. On 12 July 1948, Pandit recalled to a Russian official that in 1946 Molotov had talked about the willingness of Moscow to see the Indian Prime Minister. In October 1949, Nehru said, during a press conference in Ottawa, that 'if Stalin invites me to Moscow, I'll probably come'. On 14 January 1950, Stalin told Radhakrishnan that he was favourably disposed towards this visit. On 26 July 1951, India's Ambassador to China, K.M. Panikkar, told his Soviet counterpart, Roshchin, that Nehru would be glad to receive an invitation of the Soviet government to visit the Soviet Union in May-June 1951.[48] In a message to Stalin on 29 June 1950, Gromyko commented, 'we are favourably disposed toward Nehru's visit but the Hindus press for the official invitation of Nehru by the Soviet government'.[49] The directives to the Soviet Ambassador to China were, 'If now Nehru is willing to come to Moscow undoubtedly the Soviet government will be favourably disposed to such a wish.'[50] The top secret report dated 30 September 1952 asserted: 'As the parliamentary election campaign was on (the first general elections began in November 1951), the Hindus really expected to receive our invitation to Nehru to visit the Soviet Union—in order to raise his authority. After the end of the elections, the Hindus have not put the question any more.'[51]

Such suspicions were typical. On 29 October 1950, Gromyko wrote to Stalin that Nehru had already sent the telegram of congratulations to Stalin on the occasion of the October Revolution and the Embassy of India had asked to receive the reply as soon as possible in order to publish both telegrams in the Indian media on 7 November. The First Deputy Minister of Foreign Affairs of the USSR mentioned that 'both the text of congratulations sent by Nehru and the mentioned request of the Embassy testify that Nehru is interested to stress the strengthening of Indian-Soviet relations and to raise his prestige in India. Evidently it is especially important to him due to the coming parliamentary elections.' The Soviet Foreign Ministry recommended that Nehru's telegram of congratulations should be among the first ones to be published (on 9 November) and that a reply should be sent as early as possible (on 8 November).[52] Nevertheless, on 4 November Stalin sent a reply to Nehru. Next year the situation was the same. In his message to Stalin (3 November, 1951), Gromyko repeated the sentence about Nehru's authority and the coming elections with the recommendation that the wishes of the Indian side should be respected.[53]

The economic subsystem of bilateral relations showed signs of development. The USSR took part in the International Industrial Fair organized in Bombay in December 1951 (it was first such event to be held in India). In their message to Stalin (8 July 1951), Gromyko and M.A. Men'shikov pointed out that a prestigious place—opposite to the main entrance—was given to the Soviet stall.[54] On 21 August 1951, the Soviet of Ministers of the USSR adopted a special resolution on the USSR participation in the fair.[55]

The Soviet Union began carrying on demonstrative moves in the economic sphere. The American position helped the Soviets as from the very beginning the United States endeavoured to employ economic aid as a means of compelling the Indian government to change the course of its foreign policy. For example, towards the end of 1950, the Indian government applied to the US asking for credits necessary to buy foodgrains but the US Congress dithered over the request. The Kremlin decision to provide grain to India (the Soviet Ambassador to India was not even informed of this move) only contributed to getting things moving in the US in favour of India.

The most serious irritant in Soviet-Indian relations was linked to leftist forces in India. Moscow was greatly disturbed by the attitude of the Indian government to them. In its turn, the Indian leaders were annoyed by the Soviet support to the Indian Communists. In 1951, for example, the USSR sent 3,000 tons of newsprint to them as the Communists had informed the Soviet Embassy that 'the Indian authorities are going to stop the delivery of newsprint to progressive parties and organizations before the parliamentary elections'.[56] Soviet editions and mass media highlighted the negative characteristics of the Indian National Congress leaders. On 22 March 1952, Radhakrishnan devoted his entire meeting with Vyshinsky countering the criticism of a Soviet journalist (Borzenko, *Pravda*'s correspondent in India) who had attacked the Indian government and officials. The Indian Ambassador stated that such publications prevented the improvement of bilateral relations. The argument of Vyshinsky was that *Pravda* was a non-governmental newspaper and did not reflect the views of the Soviet government; he personally had not read the articles; 'unjustified malicious attacks against the Communists in India could form the journalist's certain opinion'. The discussion was going in circles: the Indian and Soviet arguments were repeated several times. It is interesting to note that after the meeting, Vyshinsky wrote in his diary: 'Borzenko wrote his articles (6 February and 18 February 1952) in a rude and pert manner that endangers our relations with India. Moreover, Novikov informed that Borzenko uses often unreliable sources, accuses the people unfoundedly, without any verification, spreads rumours.' The Soviet Foreign Minister complained that the Ministry had no authority to censor such publications. The whole report was sent to the members of the Political Bureau of the Communist Party, including Stalin.[57]

Soviet-Indian Relations in 1953-1955

By the beginning of the 1950s, the global situation was changing gradually: preparing for the final fight, both camps were desperately looking for new allies, capabilities and resources. The United States and the West in general found itself in a more favourable situation. They had more resources and more importantly a ready global infrastructure. So they spread their efforts to some Asian countries and started pulling together different military alliances. It greatly enhanced their offensive military capabilities. These developments forced the USSR to consider colonial and former colonial countries as a potential pool of resources for increasing the capabilities of the socialist camp, as a possible leverage against the might of the West. The problem for the Soviet Union was that among newly-independent countries there did not exist any structure that was likely to serve the Soviet purpose of counterpoising the West.

A new stage in the development of the Soviet society began in the mid-1950s. Social changes reverberated in Soviet foreign policy too. On the very day of Stalin's burial, the possibility of peaceful co-existence with the capitalist system was referred to from the Mausoleum tribune.[58] After the death of Stalin, the ideological barrier to contacts with new 'bourgeois' ruling elites of Asian and African countries was lowered a notch. At the same time a new phenomenon was emerging in the Afro-Asian world that later turned into the Non-Aligned Movement.

Nehru emerged as one of the founders of the 'Bandung Spirit' and its precursor, the *Panch Shila*. The five principles did not pitch the non-aligned countries against the Western countries (though to start with the West—for example Dulles—perceived it in a very negative way and did not conceal its attitude that made the Soviet task that much easier), but they drew a distinction between the West and Afro-Asian World, and it immediately allowed the Soviet Union to gain a footing. Though it was not clear to the USSR as to what opportunities lay in store, the Soviet Union nevertheless decided to explore the possibilities and to play on the negative Western reaction that had slightly antagonized the members of the emerging movement which had aspirations to become the world's Third Force. As India became an embodiment of the yet-to-be-born NAM and an incarnation of the Third Force, the Soviet Union's new foreign policy begun in 1953 signalled a gradual convergence with India's foreign policy.

The USSR proved to be much more flexible than the USA. The Republican administration of Dwight D. Eisenhower (1953-60) still followed the blunt and rigid tactics of 'bipolarity', supplementing the 'containment of Communism' policy with that of the 'roll back of Communism'. Accordingly, the United States intensified its political, military, diplomatic and economic interference in Asian affairs. The White House fomented military alliances on the Southern sides of the world's socialist system, such as the South-East Asia Treaty Organization (SEATO) and the Baghdad pact (renamed CENTO after 1959). At the same time American strategists initiated moves for the formation of such military organizations as the North-East Asia Treaty Organization, the Panmalaya Union (for the countries of South-East Asia). The American plan of encircling both the USSR and China from all sides was to include India and Pakistan in a 'collective defence' of Hindustan 'from the Communist threat'. Secretary of State Dulles and Vice President Richard Nixon came to India to discuss these problems in 1953, but India rejected their plans. Dulles would not even comment on the outcome of his talks with the Indian government. Nixon demanded, on his return from visits to India and Pakistan, that the US should offer military assistance to Pakistan as a counter force to the neutralism of Nehru. By the end of 1953, it became clear that the US had chosen to collaborate with Pakistan. In May 1954, US-Pakistan bilateral military agreement was concluded. In September 1954, Pakistan was inducted into SEATO and, in February 1955, into the Baghdad Pact. When, in February 1954, the Indian Prime Minister turned down Eisenhower's offer of supplying military assistance to India as well, Soviet Foreign Minister Molotov commented that, 'it was an adequate answer'.[59]

The political situation in South Asia had undergone a basic change. Pakistan, by becoming a military ally of the most powerful capitalist state became a real threat for India. Delhi's ruling circles consequently made concerted efforts to develop friendly relations first of all with the USSR and China and then, with the rest of the Socialist countries. It was in the mid-1950s that India's foreign policy decidedly changed its course from the position of neutralism to that of 'positive neutralism'. Its policy was founded on the principles of non-participation in military blocs and not allowing any military bases on its territory, liquidating colonialism, developing collaboration and peaceful co-existence of states enjoying equal rights. The most important steps in that direction were the conclusion with China in April 1954 of a treaty on Tibet based on the five principles of peaceful co-existence and an active participation in the Bandung Conference in April 1955.

India's ruling circle refused to believe the 'Northern danger' and felt that joining any military alliance would handicap India's political independence and economic self-sufficiency, and might bring the Cold War closer to its borders. Indian conservative organizations (the Jana Sangh, for example) proclaimed that Pakistan should be annexed. This party even opposed the idea of developing regular relations with the US after the conclusion of the US-Pakistan military alliance. On the contrary, Soviet-Indian relations began improving with every passing day. In 1954, co-operation between the two countries on many international issues began on a large scale. It was under these circumstances that the Indian government changed its attitude to events in Indo-China and began supporting actively the Democratic Republic of Vietnam. Thus, in the beginning of 1954, India forbade transportation of French troops to Indo-China, through its air-space. In February, Nehru issued an appeal to stop the fighting in Indo-China and declared that 'it would be especially awful if the world war begins and nobody is able to stop it'.[60] The United States reaction to the appeal was negative, the Soviet response positive. Nehru's suggestions about putting an end to the conflict were presented in the official summary of the Colombo Conference of South-East Asian Prime Ministers in April-May 1954. The Conference was convened at the Indian Prime Minister's initiative to discuss the problems of Indo-China. The Soviet government was kindly disposed towards Nehru's suggestions. During talks with the Soviet Foreign Minister on 13 March 1954, and subsequently on 19 April, the Indian Ambassador to the USSR, K.P.S. Menon vehemently attacked the US stand on Indo-China: 'Dulles is undermining the Geneva Conference'. According to him, India especially had a negative attitude to the 'defensive pact' in South-East Asia, 'due to fundamental principles and its own interests. . . . The struggle in Indo-China is the struggle for national liberation, and the proposed alliances are in reality the alliances of colonial powers with their puppets.'[61]

India was not officially represented in the Geneva Conference of 1954, Krishna Menon went there only as Nehru's special envoy. On 26 June 1954, a letter from Nehru was passed to Molotov in which he praised the Soviet Foreign Ministry for the role played in the Conference and thanked him for the attention given to Krishna Menon.[62] In his next message on 24 July 1954, the day when the agreement on a ceasefire was concluded, Nehru again praised the Soviet Minister and stressed that 'India can agree to the invitation to participate in three Commissions on Indo-China as a Chairman. We suggest to have the first meeting in Delhi on 1 August.'[63] In December, Krishna Menon complained to the Soviet Foreign Ministry that the United States was dissatisfied with the justness and objectiveness of the International Supervisory Commissions on Indo-China.[64]

The Soviet and Indian stand on disarmament were very similar. Both countries bitterly criticized the United States for the explosion of a hydrogen bomb.[65] In 1954, the UN Commission on disarmament resumed discussions. Great Britain that suggested that the US, the

USSR, Canada, Great Britain and France should be included in the subcommittee to consider the concrete aspects of arms reduction and prohibition of atomic weapons. The Soviet Union called it 'a one-sided approach' and proposed to include the PRC, India and Czechoslovakia also.[66] Moscow began supporting Delhi on the issue of regional security. On 13 March 1954, Molotov declared that 'the Soviet Union understands India's position on this problem, we have taken and shall take all necessary steps to keep Pakistan from dangerous actions made by the pressure of the United States'.[67] The Indian Ambassador to the USSR had plenty of reason to declare on 29 December 1954, that 'during last two years we have witnessed the considerable rapprochement of India and the Soviet Union, and now we understand each other much better than in the past'.[68]

During this time Soviet-Indian economic relations began developing. In December 1953, the first bilateral trade agreement was concluded in Delhi. Simultaneously the Soviet trade representation was open in India and the USSR agreed to provide technical assistance to India. In September 1954, Moscow pledged funds for the construction of the Bhilai steel mill. Indian ruling circle considered collaboration with the USSR to be an essential condition for the development of their national economy and for accelerating the industrialization of India. Western powers and international financial organizations in the mid-1950s were opposed to the development of heavy industry in the Afro-Asian world; the reason was evidently their reluctance to transform the agrarian structure and raw materials supplier role of Third World economies into something more equitable. Besides they insisted that industrialization of the developing world was far too expensive and not practical from the point of view of economic effectiveness. For India, however, the development of heavy industries was more a political objective since it strengthened national independence. Thus, the agreement with the Soviet Union to provide aid in this sphere was greeted practically by all political parties.

On 2 February 1955, a Soviet-Indian agreement on the construction of the Bhilai steel mill was signed. It should be noted that India agreed to the Soviet Union's offer of collaboration only after the Western powers had either recanted from this project or had demanded quite unfavourable terms. The plant w-s to produce 1 million ton of steel annually, roughly equal to the entire production of steel all over India at that time. Economic collaboration between the Soviet Union and India thus received a fillip. That agreement was in fact the first venture of overcoming the capitalist countries' monopoly in the sphere of economic and financial deals with developing countries. United States was naturally sharply critical, but it ultimately decided to reconsider its position and to increase its assistance to India.

Some characteristic features of the Soviet-Indian cooperation were: (1) Soviet economic and technical aid was aimed at producing capital goods as that was the only way to help India achieve complete economic independence; (2) Soviet credits were paid back in Indian rupees used by the Soviet partners to purchase Indian goods; (3) as a rule, loans apportioned to India by the Soviet Union were given for longer terms and at lower interest rates than Western credits; (4) while construction was proceeding, Soviet experts were teaching Indian technical workers and training them to be employed in the plant under construction; and (5) Soviet economic and technical aid favoured the development of state-owned industries in India.

The year 1955 witnessed radical changes in the Soviet foreign strategy. After a period of internal readjustments in the Soviet political leadership after Stalin's death, the USSR introduced changes in its policies. In 1955, the reconstruction of the country after the war was completed, Soviet nuclear and rocket programme were on their way. The Soviet Union had reached the point when it could afford to think about less immediate tasks than survival.

In 1955, the USSR signed the Austrian State Treaty and established diplomatic relations with West Germany. Although this cannot be called the first *détente*, it certainly was the occasion when certain rules were established for Europe, and when the USSR at least started talking with its opponents after ten years of extreme mutual antipathy. A certain framework was established for East-West relations in Europe. Since nothing of that kind existed in Asia, the USSR mooted a policy for the developing world as well as India (and Egypt) became a natural choice for its implementation. Nehru's visit to the USSR and the Soviet leaders' visit to India—both in 1955—symbolized the beginning of a new phase of the bilateral relations.

NOTES

1. W.J. Barnds, *India, Pakistan and the Great Powers*, London: Pall Mall Press, 1972 ; Robert H. Donaldson, *Soviet Policy Toward India, Ideology and Strategy*, Cambridge: Harvard University Press, 1974; R. Hardgrave, *India Under Pressure*, Boulder: Westview Press, 1984; Arthur Stein, *India and the Soviet*

Union: The Nehru Era, Chicago: University of Chicago Press, 1969; R.C. Horn, *Soviet-Indian Relations: Issues and Influence*, New York: Praeger, 1982; S. Wolpert, *Roots of Confrontation in South Asia: Afghanistan, Pakistan, India and the Superpowers*, New York: Oxford University Press, 1982; T. George, Sh. Chubin and R. Litvak, *Security in Southern Asia: India and the Great Powers*, Guildford, Surrey: International Institute for Strategic Studies, Biddles Ltd., 1984.

2. One can mention works by Sushila Agarwal, Jyotsna Bakshi, Jyotirmoy Banerjee, V.S. Budhraj, Pran Chopra, V.D. Chopra, G.W. Choudhury, A.K. Damodaran, V.P. Dutt, Zafar Imam, P.N. Haksar, D.K. Joshi, Nirmala Joshi, Marish Kapur, K.D. Kapur, T.N. Kaul, D. Kaushik, Rasheeduddin Khan, M. Kulkarni, K.H. Malik, Surjit Mansingh, Girish Mishra, Sadhan Mukherjee, J.A. Naik, Neelkant, M.V. Rao, Aswini K. Ray, Sarbadhikari, Bhabani Sen Gupta, Shams-ud-Din, J. Vibhakar, etc.
3. See, for example, Yu. V. Gankovsky (ed.), *Soviet Scholars View South Asia*, Lahore: People's Publishing House, 1975.
4. G. Goroshko and V. Skosyrev, *A Birch and a Banyan-tree: Russian-Indian Relations: Yesterday, Today, and Tomorrow* (in Russian), Moscow: Slavyansky Dialog, 1999.
5. See S.I. Lounev, *Diplomacy in South Asia* (in Russian), Moscow: Nauka, 1993; S. Lunew, 'Russlands Politik Gegenuber Indien und Sudasien', in *Russland und die Dritte Welt*, Klaus Fritsche (ed.), Baden-Baden: Nomos Verlagsgesellschaft, 1996; G.K. Shirokov and S.I. Lounev, *Russia, China and India in the Modern Global Processes* (in Russian), Moscow: Moscow Public Science Foundation, 1998; S.I. Lounev and G.K. Shirokov, *Transformation of the World System: The Role of the Largest States of Eurasia* (in Russian), Moscow: Academia, 2001.
6. V.I. Lenin, *It is Better to Do Less But Better,* Sochineniya (Collected Works), 5th edition, vol. 45, p. 409.
7. I.V. Stalin, *Collected Works*, vol. 4, p. 372.
8. *The Diplomatic Archive of the Foreign Ministry of Russia*, the fund of the secretariat of V. M. Molotov, inventory no. 9, portfolio no. 768, paper-case no. 52, p. 8.
9. The translation of the letter into Russian. *The Diplomatic Archive of the Foreign Ministry of Russia*, the fund of the secretariat of V. M. Molotov, inventory no. 8, portfolio no. 530, paper-case no. 34, p. 6.
10. Ibid., p. 11.
11. The letter of J. Malik to V. M. Molotov, 27 February 1947, pp. 5-6.
12. Ibid., p. 8.
13. Ibid., p. 6.
14. G. Goroshko and V. Skosyrev, *A Birch and a Banyan-tree,* pp.14-18.
15. John Foster Dulles, Eisenhower's Secretary of State, even declared that in India, the Soviet Union 'exercise a strong influence through the interim government'. *New York Herald Tribune*, 18 January 1947.

16. *The Diplomatic Archive of the Foreign Ministry of Russia,* the fund of the secretariat of V.M. Molotov, inventory no. 9, portfolio no. 769, paper-case no. 52, pp. 55-6.
17. Jawaharlal Nehru, *Independence and After: A Collection of Speeches, 1946-1949,* New York: John Day Company, 1950, p. 257.
18. *The Diplomatic Archive of the Foreign Ministry of Russia,* the fund of the secretariat of V. M. Molotov, inventory no. 9, portfolio no. 769, paper-case no. 52, pp. 37-9.
19. Ibid., the fund of the Department of South-East Asia, inventory no. 1a, portfolio no. 14, India 821, paper-case no. 1a, p. 120.
20. Ibid., the fund of the secretariat of V.M. Molotov, inventory no. 9, portfolio no. 769, paper-case no. 52, p. 50.
21. Stalin received a brief version of the report.
22. *The Diplomatic Archive of the Foreign Ministry of Russia,* the fund of the secretariat of V. M. Molotov, inventory no. 9, portfolio no. 769, paper-case no. 52, p. 53.
23. Ibid, the fund of the secretariat of V. M. Molotov, inventory no. 9, portfolio no. 766, paper-case no. 52, pp. 1-2.
24. The Soviet party archives have the report of the first Soviet Ambassador before the Commission of the Central Committee of the party on foreign policy. K.V. Novikov blamed Stalin for not sending his condolences and declared that such behaviour had damaged the Soviet interests in India.
25. The letter of J. Malik to V.M. Molotov, 27 February 1947, p. 8.
26. *The Diplomatic Archive of the Foreign Ministry of Russia,* the fund of the secretariat of V.M. Molotov, inventory no. 9, portfolio no. 769, paper-case no. 52, pp. 53, 57.
27. Ibid., the fund of the secretariat of A. Ya. Vyshinsky, inventory no. 23a, portfolio no. 183a, paper-case no. 13, pp. 19-20.
28. Ibid., the fund of the secretariat of A. Ya. Vyshinsky, inventory no. 24, portfolio no. 204, paper-case no. 17, pp. 4-5.
29. Ibid., the fund of the secretariat of A. Ya. Vyshinsky, inventory no. 23a, portfolio no. 183a, paper-case no. 13, p. 21.
30. Ibid., the fund of the secretariat of A. Ya. Vyshinsky, inventory no. 23a, portfolio no. 183, paper-case no. 13, pp. 7-9.
31. Ibid., the fund of the secretariat of A. Ya. Vyshinsky, inventory no. 24, portfolio no. 205, paper-case no. 17, p. 57.
32. On 26 July 1951, the Indian Ambassador to China, K.M. Panikkar told his Soviet colleague Roshchin that India would like to establish closer economic ties with the USSR. The Soviet Foreign Minister received the information from his staff that, due to the Indian position, the negotiations conducted by the Soviet Ambassador to India had not yet been brought to a conclusion. *The Diplomatic Archive of the Foreign Ministry of Russia,* the fund of the Secretariat of A. Ya. Vyshinsky, inventory no. 24, portfolio no. 205, paper-case no. 17, pp. 1-5.

33. *The Diplomatic Archive of the Foreign Ministry of Russia,* the fund of the secretariat of V.M. Molotov (the diary of V.M. Molotov, 30 March 1948), inventory no. 10, India 639, paper-case no. 47, pp. 2-4; 10 February 1949, inventory no. 11, India 206, paper-case no. 14, pp. 1-2.
34. Ibid., the Fund of the South-East Asia department, inventory no. 1a, portfolio no. 13, India 820, paper-case no. 1a, pp. 1-3.
35. Having learnt of that, L. Henderson, the US Ambassador to India, uttered, 'that is the day I have been waiting for'. K.P.S. Menon, *Many Worlds: An Autobiography,* Bombay: Oxford University Press, 1965, p. 268.
36. *The Diplomatic Archive of the Foreign Ministry of Russia,* the fund of the secretariat of A. Ya. Vyshinsky, inventory no. 23a, portfolio no. 183, paper-case no. 13, pp. 1-3.
37. From January 1950, the Soviet representatives stopped attending the meetings of the Security Council in order to protest against the 'injustice' done to the PRC.
38. The message of A.A. Gromyko to Stalin (10 July 1950). *The Diplomatic Archive of the Foreign Ministry of Russia,* the fund of the secretariat of A. Ya. Vyshinsky, inventory no. 23a, portfolio no. 183, paper-case no. 13, p. 4.
39. Ibid., p. 6.
40. Dean Acheson wrote, 'I have never been able to escape wholly a childhood illusion that if the world is round, the Indians must be standing on their heads'. Dean Acheson, *Present at the Creation,* London: Hamish Mamilton, 1969, p. 420.
41. The translation is from Russian. Ibid., p. 7.
42. Ibid., p. 8.
43. Ibid., pp. 9-10.
44. *The Diplomatic Archive of the Foreign Ministry of Russia,* the fund of the secretariat of A. Ya. Vyshinsky (the diary of A. Ya. Vyshinsky), inventory no. 27, portfolio no. 185, paper-case no. 44, p. 1.
45. *The Diplomatic Archive of the Foreign Ministry of Russia,* the fund of the secretariat of A. Ya. Vyshinsky, inventory no. 24, portfolio no. 204, paper-case no. 17, pp. 3, 8.
46. Goroshko and Skosyrev, *A Birch and a Banyan-tree,* pp. 60-3.
47. Ibid., p. 70.
48. *The Diplomatic Archive of the Foreign Ministry of Russia,* the fund of the secretariat of A. Ya. Vyshinsky, inventory no. 24, portfolio no. 205, paper-case no. 17, p. 1.
49. Ibid., p. 3.
50. Ibid., p. 5.
51. Ibid., p.12.
52. Ibid., the fund of the secretariat of A. Ya. Vyshinsky, inventory no. 23a, portfolio no. 183a, paper-case no. 13, p. 13.
53. Ibid., the fund of the secretariat of A. Ya. Vyshinsky, inventory no. 24, portfolio no. 204, paper-case no. 17, p. 9.

54. Ibid., the fund of the secretariat of A. Ya. Vyshinsky, inventory no. 24, portfolio no. 205, paper-case no. 17, p. 16.
55. Ibid., p. 26.
56. The message of Vyshinsky and Men'shikov to Stalin (31 August 1951). Ibid., p. 49.
57. *The Diplomatic Archive of the Foreign Ministry of Russia*, the fund of the secretariat of A. Ya. Vyshinsky (the diary of A. Ya. Vyshinsky), inventory no. 27, portfolio no. 185, paper-case no. 44, pp. 1-4.
58. A few days before his death Stalin told his inner circle, 'I am not afraid to die, I am afraid that you'll be frightened of them.'
59. *The Diplomatic Archive of the Foreign Ministry of Russia*, the fund of the secretariat of V.M. Molotov (the diary of the Minister), inventory no. 13a, portfolio no. 189, paper-case no. 37, p. 5.
60. Ibid., p. 1.
61. Ibid., pp. 9-10.
62. Ibid., p. 18.
63. Ibid., p. 24.
64. Ibid., p. 27.
65. Ibid., p. 6.
66. Ibid., p. 11.
67. Ibid., p. 4.
68. Ibid., p. 25.

MAX-JEAN ZINS

❖ Cold War in South Asia: A Look at the British Archives on India, 1947-1971

During the formative years of India's foreign policy, Britain remained the major Western influence in South Asia. Yet, by the mid-1950s, and even more so after the Suez Canal crisis, the United States had edged past London. A 1958 dispatch of the United Kingdom High Commissioner (UKHC) in India underlined this transition. Indicating that the British economic assistance to India has to be 'clearly limited', the UKHC wrote without apparent regret that: 'our material power and influence in international and particularly in Asian Affairs is not as great as it used to be, but the improvement in relations between India and America is very welcome, for the Western World as a whole can only stand to gain from it'.[1] From being a foremost actor in the field of international relations in South Asia, the United Kingdom became a more modest observer. Nevertheless, the analyses of its diplomats continued to be acute and perceptive. Through their eyes, we will also try and focus our attention on the Sino-Indian conflict of 1962 and on the 1971 Bangladesh war.

Alleviating the Post-Independence Anxieties

One has to first thoroughly investigate the main objectives of the British diplomacy, the worries London may have had about their fulfilment, the relative feeling of serenity entertained when these worries slowly vanished, and what all this revealed about India's foreign policy. In 1947, the first aim of the British diplomacy in South Asia was to preserve London's regional assets. The Labour Party' policy allowed the United Kingdom to 'quit' India without much damage to the British prestige. According to its diplomats in New Delhi. 'India', wrote the UKHC in 1952, 'regards the transfer of power in 1947 as a wise and generous action on Britain's part and appreciate the policy of the United Kingdom in relations to its colonies'.[2] Not without paternalism, they considered that the former ruler's image in India was positive. 'The Indian attitude to us now is rather like that of the Americans and the Irish on the morrow of their independence; they condemn us and disapprove of us officially and in public, but privately and personally, respect and even rather like us. . . . One day the Indians may be prepared to admit what British rule did for them, much as we are now prepared to admit what Roman rule did for us.'[3] It contrasted with France that Indians saw as 'the symbol of an outmoded imperialism'.[4] Indians generally did not mince words about the Americans either, the Secretary General of the Ministry of External Affairs, Girija Shankar Bajpai complained, for instance, about their 'arrogance'.[5] Krishna Menon disparagingly told the UKHC in Delhi that they were 'newcomers, naive, impulsive, inexperimented'[6] and dealt with India in an 'intolerable manner'.[7]

London wanted this asset to serve the interest of the 'free world'. For General Claude Auchinleck, then Commander-in-Chief of the Indian army, the geo-strategic position of India constituted a decisive factor. 'Should India be unfriendly or liable to be influenced by a power, such as Russia, China or Japan, hostile to the British Commonwealth, our strategic position in the Indian Ocean would become untenable and our communications with New Zealand and Australia most insecure.'[8] However, it was vis-à-vis the Soviet Union that the threat perception was the most intense. It figured prominently in an unusually long note entitled 'The Russian menace to India', drafted at the end of 1947 by the Far Eastern Section and the Middle Eastern Section of the FO, with the help of the Russian Section.[9] The Chinese Revolution added its own threat in 1949. In 1951, the UKHC in Delhi wrote: 'It is vital to the West that India should be denied to the Communists. If India were to slip into complete isolation, the field would be left open to communism: it is, therefore, imperative to prevent such isolation, and it has been the aim of British policy to create steadily closer association for this reason.'[10] In 1952, he insisted again, 'Our major object must be to keep India from communism and, if possible, to wean her more firmly on our side.'[11]

We were at the beginning of the Cold War and there is, indeed, nothing unexpected in this global vision. As regard denying India to the Communists, it is important to note that it was formulated in a negative form. London did not entertain high expectations about India playing an active role in the defence of the 'free world'. The British were more modest, they just hoped that India would not favour the

Communist bloc, i.e. that India would play at best a neutral or a passive role in the East-West confrontation. The UKHC in Delhi explained this viewpoint in a letter addressed to the Secretary of State of the Commonwealth Relations Office (CRO) in 1952:

> The crux of the problem . . . is really that India is not prepared to face up to the realities of the international scene or to contribute to the common defence burden of the free world. In spite of considerable development to Nehru's ideas towards greater realism, he persists in his policy of neutrality and eludes himself that India can hope to escape the designs of the aggressive communist policy. He has no longer the same illusion as in 1947 about the dangers of communism expansion but is still not prepared to take any active part with others in defending his country against them.[12]

Indeed, London seemed to think that it would be unrealistic and even counterproductive to ask India to do more in favour of the West, like joining a Western military pact. As the UKHC said, 'the Indian government have in their power to make it much worse and much more damaging to our own interest'. Pragmatically he added: 'in the set of circumstances, I do not think there is any alternative to the policy of patience and forbearance which I have advocated, however galling and irritating this has often been, accompanied by continued efforts on our part on suitable occasion to leave her no doubt of her shortcomings and induce more realistic and cooperative policies'. As the Prime Minister Anthony Eden summed it up in his memoirs: 'If they [the Indians] could not be with us, we must not put them against us.'[13] In so doing, the British were convinced that they were taking the best line to promote their own national interest:

> In determining what course of action are appropriate for meeting open hostility with which India confronts us on so many colonial matters, we must never forget the importance of our being able to influence Indian foreign policy, since in some areas she carries great weight and can play a useful role. . . . A co-operative India is also of great importance to the health of the sterling area and to our own commercial interests. Unsatisfactory though India's anti-colonial attitude may be . . . self interest demands that our own interests in the colonial field should be so conducted as to minimise the area of friction.[14]

This vision contrasted with the more blunt American approach of 'who is not with us, is against us'. The Americans disregarded India's neutralism. Indian diplomats indeed complained more than once about the US political perception of their policy. Thus, Bajpai told the UKHC in Delhi that 'he [Bajpai] was one of the best friends Americans had in this country', but also confided that 'it was [in his view] futile for America to expect India and other Asian nations to approach the communist problem in Asia in exactly the same way as the problem had been approached with American assistance in Western Europe'. The UKHC commented: 'I am afraid that Bajpai's remark to me truly reflects Indian opinion and I have heard much the same story from Cabinet ministers including Rajaji, from parliamentarians and from pressmen.'[15] Even if British diplomats generally deplored India's lack of enthusiasm for the Western diplomacy, they did not fail to criticize their American colleagues for overemphasizing the damage caused by India's external policy. For example, in 1949, the UKHC in India did not think that 'some Asian equivalent of the Marshall plan' would be 'the only practicable solution' to help India face communism or to become 'an effective bastion against communism in Asia'.[16] In 1951 again, the Foreign Office (FO) tempered a dispatch of the UKHC in Delhi echoing the American perception. A comment in the margin of the dispatch said:

> There is no doubt that Nehru is firmly opposed to communism and has given up hope that the China's brand may turn out to be different from the Russian. He advocates 'neutralism' out of a desire to see 'Asia for the Asians' and not as a result of any policy of balance and counterbalance in his attitude to East and West. I cannot recall any case where Nehru has taken positive steps to obstruct Western policy in South East Asia: cf. the lack of criticism by him of our action in Malaya and Indo-China. If there is anything he can be accused in this respect, it is that he just does nothing, and fails to use the great influence which he certainly has over the rest of South East Asia.[17]

India was not with the West, but also was not against it and ultimately, this was good enough for the FO.

Britain was also keen to preserve its specific interests regarding the economic interaction with India or armament sales. London distinguished between two main categories of partners/competitors for influence in India. Vis-à-vis the small competitors like France, Australia or New Zealand, there was no significant British anxiety. These countries were not serious rivals and London was even ready to facilitate their relations with India. For instance, British diplomacy, without having any illusions about the outdated character of French colonialism in Indo-China, had nothing against helping Paris to establish a better dialogue with New Delhi on this subject. With the United States, the situation was slightly more delicate. On the one hand, the Americans were the best allies of the British and the main pillar of the Capitalist bloc against the Socialist order. On the other hand, they represented a formidable challenge to British economic interests in India. 'We . . . have constantly to bear in mind all our Commonwealth partners even if the United States does not like some of them,' Anthony Eden told his diplomats, 'and I must ask you to keep close watch on this aspect of our affairs, and not hesitate to press it on the United States.'[18] The FO archives were more explicit. In 1948, the Far Eastern Section commented on a report of the CRO:

> The part we want America to play may depend to a considerable extent on whether India and Pakistan are in the Commonwealth and her sterling area, or not. If they are, we would hope that the United States would let us make the running and in general back us up. We would in that case not want Pakistan and India to spend more dollars than necessary. But if one or both leave the sterling area, we should want the Americans to play as big a part in their national life as possible. The stronger the commercial ties established the better, for American capital indirectly would protect our own hand and, of course, keep Russians out.[19]

This last possibility nevertheless caused some worry: 'In our anxiety to reach dollar markets, it will be a great pity if we lose ground in the sub-continent which it may never be possible to regain. India and Pakistan are . . . as good a commercial risk as most other markets East of Suez and looking a bit into the future, their potential value to our export trade is something we probably can ill afford to ignore.'[20] In 1954, however, globally British diplomacy did not seem to be overly worried:

> There is no sign of American firms wishing to invest in this country. . . . Our prices and dollar discrimination have so far protected us against the Americans. . . . The main weight of American aid has been directed to the agricultural sphere and is undoubtedly contributing to an accelerate rate of economic development which will a provide larger market than would otherwise have been available.[21]

The problem engendered by the Anglo-American competition in the field of armaments is more complex. Initially, the main question for London was to maintain a balance between India and Pakistan: 'The policy as approved by the Cabinet in March 1952 was that broad parity should be maintained between India and Pakistan.' Further, supplies had to be studied on a case by case basis: 'In each case where supplies to India are in question there may be political and strategic advantages from the point of view of our relations with Pakistan in withholding supplies. These will have to be weighted against the political, strategic and economic disabilities that the withholding of supplies would impose on our relations with India. The same considerations apply, *mutatis mutandis*, to supplies to Pakistan.'[22] The difficulty was, of course, to convince Indians and Pakistanis that the parity was really respected. Yet as a principle, this concept did not create a problem. India did not object to it, as long as the buyers paid for the weapons supplied.[23] But the game became more complex when Pakistan, once it joined Western military alliances, started receiving sophisticated weapons with American financial assistance. The spirit of parity was no longer respected and India did not take it kindly. New Delhi looked for other supply sources and this in turn led Pakistan to ask for more weapons, a demand that London could not turn down without 'lamentable results'. It was not easy, in these circumstances, to 'avert Pakistan indignation and mitigate Indian resentment'.[24] This contradiction may be one of the factors explaining British lack of enthusiasm for the integration of Pakistan in the Western military pacts in Asia.

British fears regarding the future of India's foreign policy were not just a reflection of Nehru's stand, but also arose from the uncertainties of India's internal politics. During the initial years of India's independence, London was afraid that chaos or instability might develop and may favour the Communists and the Soviet Union. True, the British diplomacy underlined reassuringly that 'the Congress Party, which in effect controls the Union of India, is largely the instrument of Indian big-business'.[25] If Nehru's moderating influence was indeed appreciated—'he threw his great influence on the side of moderation in the discussions on national movements', a British diplomat who attended the New Delhi Asian Relations Conference of 1947 wrote. The same observer was nevertheless afraid of Nehru's 'naivety' towards the Communist threat, 'it passed through many minds that this Kashmiri aristocrat might be destined to fill the role of Kerensky in an Indian revolution'.[26] In 1950, the strengthening of the Congress Hindu right-wing under Vallabhbhai Patel's leadership again generated some anxiety among the British diplomacy. 'On the sphere of pure foreign policy, the effect may not be great. In regard to Indian attitude to Soviet Union, it might even be to our advantage since Sardar Patel and his group are strong opponents to communism. But in general a more narrowly nationalist trend may be expected to appear in Indian politics', noted the UKHC from Delhi.[27] Three causes of concern were to endure. The first one related to the relationship between India and Soviet Union. It is a well-known factor and will not be discussed here. The second one concerned the Indo-China interaction and the third one was the regional vision of India which shall be discussed further.

THE CHINESE PUZZLE

The Indian perception of China perplexed the British. The 1949 Chinese Revolution did not only bring about a new Communist state, it also signified the emergence of a new power in Asia, mysterious for the West but a source of potential pride for the peoples of Asia. The West had not forgotten the pride that Asia, including India, felt after the Japanese victory over the Russian troops in 1905. Could not the West think that India would have the same feeling about China's new vitality? Did not Nehru's own sister and India's Ambassador in Moscow, Vijayalakshmi Pandit, tell the Western diplomats 'to hold a high opinion' of the Chinese Communists who, she said, were more open-minded than the Russian Communists? [28] Were not the British diplomats bound to note that India was not prepared to contest the influence of China over Tibet? The Indian Ambassador in Beijing, K.M. Panikkar, 'left me with the clear impression that the liberation of Tibet by the present Chinese government would not be treated by the Indian government as a very serious development', the UK Ambassador in China wrote.[29] C. Rajagopalachari, a conservative leader of the Congress Party, however, said he was 'rather gloomily about the future prospects of Tibet' and seemed to consider that Tibet was just a diplomatic card for India.[30] G.S. Bajpai said that he was 'very sceptical' about India sending arms to Tibet.[31] Worse, in an Indian memorandum sent to the Chinese, he seemed to have confused the words suzerainty and sovereignty to define the status of Tibet vis-à-vis China, when these two notions were clearly not the same: the first one left totally open the question of an eventual autonomy of Tibet; the second one left no doubt about the fact that Tibet belonged to China.[32] British diplomacy was also very surprised by India's systematic efforts 'to act as an intermediary' between China and the West on crucial questions like the unity of China, the Korean war or Beijing's entry in the UN.[33] Of course, the British diplomats did not know that Nehru wrote to K.M. Panikkar at the same time that 'the whole cornerstone of our policy during the past few months has been friendly relations with China and we have almost fallen out with other countries because of this policy that we have pursued'.[34] But one can imagine British surprise when it was mentioned that the Indian diplomats were happy to tell them that the Chinese foreign minister did not consider India as an American agent.[35] London did not understand why the Indians stressed upon the differences between Moscow and Beijing when for the British diplomacy, the two were first and foremost communist. The UKHC in New Delhi commented: 'The Indians are prepared to clutch at any straw and hope that China will not fall completely under Moscow's sway.'[36] For London, which thought that China and India were two archrivals of Asia ('India's aim was to acquire implicitly if not explicitly some form of leadership in Asia. It was the aim of China to prevent this happening'),[37] India's attitude was mind-boggling and the only option for the West was to wait and see and hope for better times: 'The process of India's education must be mainly through the impact of events. We do everything we can to promote the process of education but it is only the action of the communist world that will complete that education, and we cannot complacently assume that communist tactics will be so clumsy in South and South East Asia as to bring any drastic change of Indian views in the short term.' [38] The third British apprehension concerned the policy of India towards its neighbours. According to London, India wanted to play a leadership role in South Asia and maybe in Asia. 'Her [India] remote aim' is to be 'accepted as the leading power if not the whole of Asia at any rate in South East Asia'.[39] This phenomenon drew the attention of British diplomacy in many ways.

On the one hand, this supposed hegemonic will of India somehow suited London. In controlling its region, India contained both Soviet and Chinese threats. It is interesting to note here that London did not criticize India's role in Nepal, Bhutan and Sikkim, even if London was aware of existing anti-Indian feelings in these countries. 'It seems that India does not want to annex Nepal by force but that she should become her satellite before very long', the UKHC in India calmly observed.[40] One can note too that London did not favour the development of internal centrifugal forces in India, even if the British had sympathy for some of them. In 1948, the decision of Sheikh Abdullah's National Conference of Kashmir to join India was analysed as 'a setback to the pro-Communist faction which favours independence'.[41] The same fundamental approach was adopted in 1953 regarding the Nagas:

> With memories of the Naga's war record, it is difficult for us not to feel some sympathy for the aspirations of those tribesmen and it is certainly flattering to learn that they would still prefer their affairs to be supervised by British political officers than by a more 'democratic' Indian regime. On the other hand this uncompromising desire for a fully independent Nagaland can do neither the Nagas themselves nor India any good and if persisted in may lead to the adoption of more extreme measures by both sides; in the long run a serious deterioration of law and order in this important frontier territory can only benefit to communists who are already alive to the potentialities of the situation.[42]

In the same vein, London was to develop in the 1950s some apprehension about the decentralized linguistic policy of Nehru for it could suit the Communists.

However, on the other hand, as seen from London, New Delhi's hegemonic policy hampered the emergence of good relations between India and Pakistan. That complicated the British diplomacy: 'Obviously the more Pakistan and India disagree, the more difficult it will be for us to keep friendship of both. And we must keep the friendship with both if we are to be instrumental in maintaining the peace, welfare and security of that broad belt of the world which stretches from the Mediterranean to the China Sea.'[43] The Indo-Pakistani tension clearly represented an obstacle to the unity of the subcontinent, a phenomenon which could be used by the USSR for its own benefit (in 1948, London nourished the hope of Pakistan and Afghanistan signing a defence agreement that India could join afterwards).[44] One can also add that London feared a kind of Indian 'Pan-Asiatism' ('we realised that Nehru is obsessed at present with the idea of Asia for the Asiatics')[45] which could favour anti-Western feelings.

There was a large gap between the anxiety expressed in the immediate post-Independence and the serenity seen five years later. In India itself, the Communist threat was under control: 'Indeed one might be reasonably optimistic about the future. . . .'[46] In the international field, India's policy appeared to the British diplomats more realistic than expected, either vis-à-vis the Communists in Asia or vis-à-vis the East-West confrontation. In Asia itself, as a specialist of the relationship between India and South-East Asia wrote, the 'unreserved intervention' of India in favour of nationalist Indonesia contrasts with the relative 'coolness' of the Indian diplomacy towards communist Vietnam, whatever personal sympathy Nehru has for Ho Chi Minh.[47] London was aware of this and even went to the extent of asking (vainly) India about a possible support for Bao Dai in

Vietnam. London also appreciated the role played by India during the Geneva Conference on Indochina. Regarding Indonesia, Britain spoke very highly of Nehru. His visit to Jakarta in June 1950 'has been most valuable. He has attempted . . . with some success to bring the Indonesian leaders down to earth and to show them that the external threat now comes not from Western colonialism but from the "new imperialism" of communism.'[48] In 1951, on the whole, Indian policy in South-East Asia looked positive for the British: '. . . the advice which India gives to Burma and Indonesia is generally sound and not without influence; and in his attitude towards Malaya, Nehru has gone away in suppressing his anti-colonial prejudices and has on occasion been surprisingly helpful'.[49] In his memoirs, Anthony Eden explained that India, like the UK 'had a concern in limiting the onward rush of communist forces' because it did not relish to see Burma and Thailand passing under communist control'.[50]

London was less apprehensive about India's Chinese policy. The British understood that supporting diplomatically China did not make India 'pro-communist' or 'pro-Chinese': 'There is no doubt that Nehru is firmly opposed to communism' and India is 'fully alive to the Chinese communist threat on the Northern frontier'.[51] If India was officially and openly sympathetic towards China, it was not because it liked its neighbour but because it feared China mainly for geo-strategic reasons. To reduce the threat from its big northern neighbour, India tried then to tame it. In other words, India adopted a 'friendly' posture towards China in the hope that this would result in China adopting 'gentlemanly' behaviour in the field of international relations and regarding the Sino-Indian border issue. A 1952 dispatch of the UKHC in Delhi illustrated the perceptiveness of British diplomats:

> India's attitude towards China represents the most complex piece in the puzzle of Indian foreign policy. It is the least easy to fathom, and presents many inconsistencies, but it is at the same time, I think, the key to the whole. I believe that the explanation is that the public declarations of the Indian government are fundamentally out of accord with their real appreciation of the position in China. I suspect that fear is really their basic motive. . . . They are horrified at the possibility of war and feel that at all cost they must avoid involvement in any clash with China. It is this that makes them so sensitive to any actions by the Americans which they fear may provoke China into a war which would bring the destruction of the whole of Asia. They are determined to bend every effort to avoid this. The only course they see for themselves is, therefore, to

cultivate and retain friendly relation with communist China, and they feel that almost any price is worth paying to achieve this.[52]

The Indian attitude *vis-à-vis* China appeared rational to the British and this rationality allayed their apprehensions.

The intriguing 'India-China Agreement on Trade and Inter-Course between Tibet Region of China and India' of 29 April 1954 was a case in point. In this agreement, New Delhi formally recognized the sovereignty of China over Tibet. At the same time, the agreement contained in its preamble the famous five principles of peaceful co-existence. Was it not a paradox to see a simple bilateral agreement containing such an important vision of international relations? At first, the British thought the five principles had been mentioned 'apparently at Chinese instance'.[53] But soon they realized, thanks to Panikkar, that 'this was not the case' and 'that the idea . . . had been the result of Indian initiative, since the government of India had wished to stress to the Chinese government that they had given up any claim to interfere in Tibetan affairs or to have "unequal" privileges'.[54] It meant that India exchanged the recognition of Chinese sovereignty over Tibet against a Chinese promise to respect the principles of peaceful co-existence. One could then understand the calculation: as India knew perfectly well that it could not solve by force its differences with China over the border, Delhi expected to persuade China to follow the five principles to solve the differences, i.e. China would not go to war to change the border status quo that New Delhi wanted to maintain. Was India chasing after rainbows? The question is debatable but it remains that India's stance looked rational.

After 1951-2, even the predictable consequences of the US-Pakistan military alliance did not seem to shake British confidence: London was convinced that India, having adopted a fundamentally moderate foreign policy, would swallow hard and would not react by entering into the Soviet orbit. This point will be discussed on the basis of the exchange of opinions that occurred between the UKHC in Delhi and the UKHC Karachi at the end of 1951 at the demand of the CRO.[55] It illustrates how London developed its external policy on the basis of its perception of India's foreign policy. On the one hand, there were those who, like Archibald Nye, the UKHC in India, did not favour the integration of Pakistan in the military Western alliances: 'A military agreement between Pakistan and the Western Powers would bring the dormant suspicions up to the surface again.' India would then multiply the gestures of independence. Delhi may try to develop its ties with the USSR and China, to strengthen a bloc of neutralist countries in Asia, to ask Nepal not to send Gurkhas to the British army, to try to isolate Pakistan by developing a more friendly relationship with Afghanistan, or even to quit the Commonwealth. Supposing a world war broke out, India would be very hesitant about joining the Western camp. This would be a pity and more so because at the moment India would be ready 'to interpret her neutrality with some flexibility' and even 'come in on the side of the Allies'. As far as the subcontinent was concerned, according to Nye, the consequence would be 'disastrous'. The Kashmir question would not find any solution for years and the new atmosphere 'might substantially increase the danger of war between India and Pakistan in times of tension'.

On the other hand, Gilbert Laithwaite, the UKHC in Karachi, thought that London could take the risk of antagonizing India. First, he argued that the Pakistani leaders wanted to forge a military alliance with the West and this would help to contain communism in the Middle East and in Muslim countries. Secondly, he stated that India would not dare to change its world-view to the extent of shifting towards the Communist bloc. Laithwaite emphasized that his colleague in Delhi himself said that 'the Indian attitude is fundamentally one of sympathy with the ideals of the democratic countries', that 'the development of Indian foreign policy since 1947 has been a slow process of increasing readiness to understand the menace of communism and willingness to appreciate the Western point of view', that 'on the basis of existing relations there is no risk of India's joining the Communist side' and 'that there is indeed a chance that her neutrality at the beginning of a war might be modified in favour of the democracies and eventually transformed into active belligerence on our side'. In these conditions, the UKHC in Karachi asserted that it would be inconceivable ('indeed, I would say impossible') to 'permanently sterilise Pakistan' under the pretext of raising a 'misunderstanding' in India. In this case, 'the disadvantage that Indian neutrality would impose on us' would be 'greatly aggravated'.

This debate is particularly telling. In particular, it indicated that London was very much aware of the negative consequences of a military agreement between Pakistan and the Western powers for the Indian subcontinent. Indian distrust towards the West was bound to increase. As Nye wrote,

> One of the fundamental ingredients in [this] distrust is the fear that the Western powers may allow strategic requirements to determine their policies in South Asia and that this may ultimately lead to plans inconsistent with the independence of the area from European predominance. There is also a growing fear that, with the widening rift between the Western world and the Communist bloc, the Western Powers might involve South Asia in another world war. . . . It would be thought that Western relations with the sub-continent would increasingly be dominated by strategic objectives with bias against India.

Nevertheless, London banked on New Delhi's moderation in considering establishing military ties with Pakistan, concluding that India in the end would not adopt a too strong anti-Western posture. Indeed, what happened suggests that Laithwaite won his bet but that many of the negative consequences foreseen by Nye also occurred: the Kashmir question stayed unresolved and war between Pakistan and India became a recurrent threat.

Red Stars Conflicting over South Asia

It is a well-established fact that China kept on contesting the kind of leadership USSR tried to establish over the world because of its competition with the USA. This indeed largely determined China's anti-Indian posture at the end of the 1950s. The 1962 Sino-Indian war was much more than a mere bilateral friction and has to be placed in a global context for a better understanding. It opened a new historical phase in the Cold War and cleared the way for a new configuration of international forces, illustrated in 1971 by the Bangladesh war. Even if the UK had lost a lot of its traditional influence after the mid-1950s, London continued to be one of the best diplomatic observers in South Asia. The entry of China into the regional game did not alter this. London, unlike Washington and Paris, had established diplomatic relations with the PRC and remained as one of the best-informed world capitals on China. This confers special relevance to the FO archives. I shall use them to try and understand some aspects concerning the India-China dispute of 1962.

My argument starts from the changes which occurred in the Soviet Union at the beginning of the 1950s. Everything happened as if the Soviet society, exhausted by the Second World War and the impact of Stalinism, wanted to live a little better, a little more 'normally'. The deafening echo of the Western economic recovery also had its own impact on the Soviet political élite, probably more fascinated by the West than they were prepared to admit. Nehru seemed to perceive this when he insisted in his talks with British leaders on 'the reorganization in the Russian economy and the decision of Malenkov to raise the standard of living of the Russian people', something that could turn 'to the advantage of the West'.[56] The Indians observed, on the occasion of Nehru's visit to Moscow, that USSR did its best to develop its industrial activity 'including consumer side', according to the British representation in Washington.[57] The British Embassy in Moscow seemed to share the same view when it commented on the necessity for Khrushchev to follow what could be termed as the 'policy of the bacon'. 'He . . . must surely feel himself under a powerful compulsion to bring home; if not the bacon, at least something which can be represented as much.'[58] This rising expectation of the Soviet people had many important consequences in the field of defence and foreign policy. To respond to it implied less spending in armaments. As Nehru said, 'what Russia now wanted was fifteen or twenty years of peace to built their industry . . . to a level comparable to that which obtained in the West'.[59] This required an atmosphere of détente with the USA. Yet at the same time, Moscow did not want to give up defence parity with Washington; the only option open for the Soviet Union was to rely on the 'equilibrium of terror' that its new nuclear capability provided. The nuclear deterrence allowed Moscow to solve the contradiction affecting Soviet policy in the 1950s: thanks to the atomic umbrella—Moscow hoped that the negotiations with Washington would make its financial costs affordable—USSR could hope not to spend too much on defence and to overcome its American enemy politically and ideologically in the long run. Moscow's vision of the class struggle at the international level led it to think that America and its allies, as imperialist powers, would be gradually isolated by the inescapable emergence of anti-imperialist forces. In the early 1950s, the decolonization process seemed to validate this scenario (conceived as a 'theory'). Peaceful co-existence and nuclear non-proliferation became the two main pillars of Khrushchev's foreign policy. In this framework, India looked like the archetype of the 'good' country, being non-aligned, peaceful—including towards China—and opposed to nuclear proliferation. The 'major change in Soviet thinking'[60] underlined by the Indian diplomacy in the mid-1950s was at the basis of 'the unfortunate coincidence of Indian and Russian interest' that irritated Western diplomacy.[61] The 'change' happened more on the Soviet side than on the Indian side. It is not India that was 'pro-Soviet', but the USSR that had become 'pro-Indian'.[62]

The problem for Moscow was that Beijing could neither accept the Soviet vision nor its historical implication. The idea of an international system consisting of a series of concentric alliances around the USSR—Moscow at the centre, then China in Asia and the European satellites, then the non-aligned countries, followed by the countries fighting for their independence and the different communist parties of the capitalist world, etc.—could not satisfy Communist China's national aspirations. The first Chinese criticism was focused on the theory of peaceful co-existence. Beijing saw this as 'revisionist', meaning that China was by contrast the new revolutionary centre of the world. The second criticism was directed against the notion of balance of terror. Beijing did not like the idea of the Soviet Union discussing the nuclear destiny of the world with the USA. In 1959, the Northern Department of the FO underlined, in these terms, the reasons why Khrushchev was probably very happy with his visit to the USA: his visit meant 'the US recognition of the fact that there are only two great powers in the world today, that the Soviet Union is one of them, that she is equal to the USA, and that it is only a step to some total division of the world into two spheres of influence with the US-recognizing the status quo of the Soviet bloc'.[63] Consequently, Khrushchev's insistence on peace during his visit to Washington was analysed by the British as 'an admonition to the Chinese'.[64] For China, the USSR was not only a 'revisionist' state but also an 'hegemonic' state. The Maoist theory of the 'double hegemony' in the field of class struggle appeared to be a direct replica of the 'revisionist' one in the field of international relations.

INDIA AT THE INTERSECTION OF CONFLICTING STRATEGIES

India was precisely and dangerously located at the intersection of the Chinese and Soviet conflicting strategies. Praised by Moscow, New Delhi was for the very same reasons disliked by Beijing. After the mid-1950s, the deteriorating Sino-Indian relations ran parallel with the erosion in Sino-Soviet relations. Year after year, but without connecting both the processes, British dispatches from Delhi, Karachi, Moscow and Beijing pointed out this reality. In 1953, British diplomats in Beijing suggested that the Sino-Indian relations 'were cooling off'[65] and that Nehru 'was becoming conscious of the real nature of the new China and its implication for India'.[66] At the same time, their colleagues in Moscow noted with interest and surprise that Moscow had adopted a more moderate approach than China towards the sale of American weapons to Pakistan; Moscow insisted upon a East-West rapprochement but Beijing put more emphasis on the necessity to unite the people of Asia.[67] They commented that 'there have been a number of signs in the last few months of the increased attention paid by the Soviet authorities to the improvement and widening of Indo-Soviet relations', a phenomena that seemed to accompany a new competition between Moscow and Beijing in the sphere of cultural activities in India.[68] They noticed that the new Soviet Ambassador in Beijing, in his accreditation speech, made 'no reference to Russian aid: he merely conveys the Russian wish that China will attain now successes in industrialisation, etc.' and that Mao Zedong in return contented himself with pronouncing a bland discourse on 'mutual aid and co-operation'.[69]

In 1954, British diplomats in New Delhi and Beijing discerned some problems behind the official '*Hindi-Chini Bhai Bhai*' discourse. At the end of Zhou Enlai's visit to India, they concluded that 'the points of difference in approach between the two Prime Ministers seem to have been almost as numerous as the points of agreement in practice and this has not, I think, escaped the more perceptive Indian commentators'.[70] During the same period, some Indian central ministers mentioned their increasing distrust towards China.[71] In August, for the first time, British diplomats in Beijing conveyed 'the strong impression that an important evolution in Chinese foreign policy is taking place and that central policy decisions have already been taken'.[72] The FO officials concurred, proof of it was China's behaviour during the Geneva Conference on Indo-China: 'It seems that what we have happening before us now is an evolution of Chinese foreign policy away from exclusive concentration on the Soviet bloc and towards increased connections with the West.' The FO concluded that the epoch of China 'leaning on one side' may end and that the Sino-Soviet friendship could be just 'another mask' of the Chinese external policy.[73] At the same time, they notice that the relationship between India and China was no longer totally smooth. They concluded that after his visit to China 'Nehru may have disappointed the Chinese to some extent'.[74]

It is well known that 1955 was an epoch-making year for Indo-Soviet relations. Comparatively speaking, it was not such a good year for Sino-Soviet relations in the commercial and economic field. British diplomats tried to find an explanation for this:

It should not be overlooked that in spite of the ideological-political ties now uniting the USSR and China, many Russian communists must regard the prospect of a highly industrialised and militarised 600-1000 million strong Chinese neighbour with serious misgivings and therefore tend to oppose the diversion to China of large supplies of goods and equipment from the overstrained Soviet economy at the present critical phase of development.[75]

Did China develop a certain rancour vis-à-vis Moscow, a feeling that could not lead Beijing to be more sympathetic towards India? Whatever may be the reason, Moscow started defending itself against the veiled Chinese accusation of 'revisionism', with Khrushchev stating that 'anyone who mistakes our smile for a withdrawal from the policy of Marx and Lenin is making a mistake'.[76] Indian diplomats, while conveying to their British colleagues that the Chinese did not seem to appreciate the increasing influence of Russia in China, did not hide anymore their suspicion about Beijing's intentions regarding the Sino-Indian border.[77] The rift between Moscow and Beijing became more open in the wake of the twentieth congress of the Communist Party of the Soviet Union. According to the British Embassy in Moscow, the Soviet Minister of External Affairs told the US Ambassador 'that the Chinese, in common with the new revolutionaries, were inclined to be over-excitable and needed to be restrained'.[78] India's discomfort vis-à-vis the Chinese external policy was now palpable for the UKHC in New Delhi: 'The Indians are prepared to be more openly worried about Chinese intentions that they have allowed themselves to appear in recent years.'[79] Events slowly moved towards the Sino-Indian war of 1962.

The analysis of the FO archives led us to underline the weakness of the Indian diplomatic position and its lack of realism. The border dispute between India and China focused essentially on two areas: the eastern sector and the western sector, the latter being the most important for China's control over Tibet. From the beginning, the Indian diplomacy adopted more or less the position that nothing was negotiable. Nehru proclaimed this publicly in the parliament, reducing by the same token his margin of manoeuvre. Yet, the Indian leaders knew that the balance of power was not in their favour. And they did not hide this fact from the British. Some Indian diplomats told their British counterparts that India was in a ratio of '1:7' vis-à-vis China.[80] Nor was the military leadership more optimistic. According to the Chief of the Indian army, General K.S. Thimayya, the actual McMahon

Line was 'militarily indefensible'[81] and in Ladakh, the General considered that 'it would now need a major military operation to recover it. So from the Indian point of view, it is a liability rather than an asset.'[82] Diplomats were even less diplomatic: 'there is little or nothing that the Indians can do to prevent this', N.R. Pillai, the Secretary-General of the Ministry of External Affairs said to the UKHC.[83] In spite of recognizing this state of inferiority, the Indian leadership did not offer any realistic negotiating propositions to the Chinese. Basically, India remained inflexible and Nehru even gave the order to the Indian army to move forward wherever it could.

What is more surprising is that officials in India even believed that an agreement with China was at hand. Nearly everyone dealing with the issue in India confided to the British that the Chinese would be ready to exchange their claim in the eastern sector for their claim in the western sector (in other words validating the McMahon Line in exchange for the Aksai Chin). Furthermore, it would be the only realistic, if not satisfying, solution to the border dispute. In November 1959, N.R. Pillai said to the UKHC that most of his colleagues were of the opinion that China's aim was to get such an 'exchange' of territory.[84] In April 1960, India's Vice President, Dr. Sarvepalli Radhakrishnan, qualified this bargain as a 'sensible compromise'.[85] The same month, Pillai reaffirmed 'that the Chinese would be prepared for some sort of a deal on the basis of the status quo in the NEFA and other areas for an Indian concession in Ladakh.'[86] Sarvepalli Gopal, Director of the Historical Division of the Ministry of External Affairs in India from 1954 to 1966, said this was the objective of the Chinese.[87] In July 1960, the UKHC in Delhi told London that Krishna Menon, the Indian Defence Minister,

> informed me with this characteristic brutal frankness that the problem could be only settled by 'horse trading' and the Vice-President confided to me in more diplomatic, if feebler language, that if the Chinese would yield Indian 'the shadow' of sovereignty in Ladakh, the Indians should yield to the Chinese the substance of administrative military control there. Mr Menon indicated to me that Mr Nehru argues with this view. . . .

Even the army people underlined that Ladakh was uninhabited and without any economic value.[88] In the wake of the Chinese offensive of October 1962, an Indian diplomat continued to say that a disputed territories exchange could have been the basis of a dialogue, that Nehru was prepared to support this idea and that 'the possible surrender of territory in Ladakh might have been a possible deal for India'.[89] The British conviction was clear, 'Our assessment—based on a fair amount of evidence—remains that the Chinese territorial aspirations in any eventual settlement are confined to Ladakh, and that they would be prepared to recognize the McMahon Line in NEFA'.[90]

Why, then, such an obstinacy on the part of India, something that allowed China to isolate India diplomatically in its own region (China systematically signed border agreements with Pakistan, Nepal, Bhutan and Burma), to defeat the Indian army and to impose finally a *de facto* border worse than the one India could have obtained through a compromise? The same haunting explanation for the Indian official stubbornness runs through the reports in the archives: according to the Indian diplomats—at least that was what they said to the British—the Indian public opinion would not accept the kind of realistic compromise envisaged in private by Indian leaders.[91] For any keen observer aware of Indian domestic politics, the argument is not surprising. One has to remember that Nehru's policy was then strongly criticized by the Jan Sangh, by a part of the Congress right-wing and also by the Socialist Party. All these elements would have without any doubt denounced with the same virulence any attempt to find a realistic compromise with China as a betrayal of India's national interests. It is also true that Nehru, facing this hostile campaign and to some extent trapped by his own policy, decided precisely to offer his public opinion the image of a firm leader, strongly attached to the integrity of Indian territory. Thus, the argument of the public opinion given by Indian diplomats to the British sounds plausible, provided it is understood that this public opinion has been politically prepared to express its feelings by the very same people who said they were following it.

Under these circumstances, the British diplomats were not surprised by their Indian colleagues' statements that Nehru never envisaged seriously to negotiate. The Joint Secretary in the Ministry of External Affairs, K.L. Mehta, said: 'Nehru could not have intended "negotiating" with the Chinese for he did not study the detailed brief about the areas under dispute prepared for him by his advisers before the meetings.'[92] True, the Chinese themselves, according to the Indians, did not come to the table with appropriate maps. Everything happened, indeed, as if both parties were giving more importance to principles than to concrete facts. The dispute's symbolic dimension then became essential and the conflict was consequently conceived in moral terms. The UKHC in Delhi was told that 'China can probably never again be trusted'. He added that Nehru 'observed to me a few days ago that the Chinese have a highly developed superiority complex and that he thinks this is the fundamental explanation of recent Chinese behaviour'.[93] Pillai said that 'as long as they [the Chinese] remained completely unrepentant, then could be no question of the government of India making any concession'.[94] It is clear, however, that the Chinese had no inclination to repent. On the contrary, the Chinese Ambassador in Moscow told his Pakistani counterpart that Indians were becoming 'mad' and they were going to teach them 'a lesson'.[95] It was 'repentance' versus 'lesson'. The British commented: 'The Chinese and the Indians are well-matched when it is a question of observation and pride. It is just mutual preoccupation with face which makes the border dispute so dangerous.'[96] In fact, a new balance of power was emerging in the subcontinent.

The rift between Moscow and Beijing would open a space for the emergence of two new strategic axes, New Delhi-Moscow and Washington-Beijing. Fundamentally, the Sino-Indian war embarrassed Moscow. Initially, Moscow did not say much and its silence was interpreted by the British as more favourable to Beijing than to New Delhi. India seemed to share this view. Nehru himself, in October 1962, told the UKHC in Delhi that the Soviet diplomacy tried 'to put the Chinese behaviour in less unfavourable light' as far as the border issue was concerned.[97] But the Soviet leadership at the same time was against any Chinese military action. 'The Indians assume that the Soviet Union cannot wish to see Chinese action drive India into the Western camp', observed the UKHC in Delhi, adding, 'yet this is what may happen unless Sino-Indian tensions abates'.[98] In other words, Moscow faced a dilemma—not to antagonize China without displeasing India. In following such a line, they would in fact annoy China more than India. In openly and loudly supporting Moscow in each world crisis (Budapest, 1956; the U2 incident and the Paris Summit Conference, 1960; the Cuba missile crisis, 1962), Beijing had sent in fact an implicit message to the USSR: the Soviets should favour their Communist brothers, not their vacillating capitalist friends like India. The Western capitals shared with the Indian diplomats this view and partly analysed the attitude of Moscow during the Cuban crisis as a result of Chinese pressure upon Khrushchev.[99] According to the British, 'the Indians are at the moment attracted by the theory that the Chinese may have moved at that time on the theory that the Russians were likely to get into serious trouble with the Americans over Berlin, Cuba, etc.

and therefore would not be able to afford to take a strong line with the Chinese if the latter attacked India'.[100] However, the fact was that Moscow would stick to its détente policy and would slowly adopt a line more and more sympathetic to India. This decision would have at least two very important long-term consequences.

On the one hand, a durable sense of 'friendship' emerged between Delhi and Moscow. In a way, India felt protected by the USSR against China. This would allow it not to join any Western alliance and to stick to its non-aligned policy. The essence of this phenomenon was perceived quite early by N.R. Pillai, who had explained to the British as early as in 1959 that

> it was a fact that if the communist bloc had shown a solid front in supporting China, India would not have been able to stick to non-alignment. The Russians had seen that. They had also seen that if India abandoned non-alignment it will not be to the interest either of Russia or of the communist bloc. The Russian's apparent objectivity towards the dispute and their failure to give full support to the Chinese was, therefore, the policy which suited the interests of the communist bloc as a whole.[101]

The 1962 India-China war confirmed this approach with a slight change: as Moscow finally sided with India, there would be no more questions of 'the interests of the communist bloc as a whole'. A new phase of the Cold War opened, underscored by the Sino-Soviet split. The 'Indo-Soviet connection' consequently strengthened.

On the other hand, the Sino-Soviet relationship deteriorated to a point of no return. China became a kind of a free electron in the international sphere whose force of attraction could be picked up by any interested power provided it was anti-Soviet.[102] The evolution opened inevitably a new space for Western strategy. But in the midst of the 1962 war, the West considered that India had to be defended against China and that the fight between these two countries was a struggle between 'the largest of the free world democracies' and the symbol of Communism. This was exactly how London perceived the US policy: 'The United States Government was concerned first and foremost with the enhancement of Chinese Communist prestige that might result from a military defeat upon India. A refusal to come to the aid of India in this crisis would, it was argued, bring into doubt the basic posture of the Kennedy administration towards Communist aggression.'[103] This view would last for some years and consequently China continued to be perceived as the enemy number one in Asia.

The nuisance value of China for the Soviet Union was nevertheless acknowledged. According to the British Ambassador in Moscow, the Sino-Soviet split 'must increase incalculably the strain under which Khrushchev pursues his tactics. Always he must be concerned to ensure that the Chinese insinuations find no credence among his own supporters. . . . And always he must be aware of an extra pressure to prove the correctness of his methods by achieving practical and visible results.'[104] Contrary to Washington, Pakistan had, by the time of the Sino-Indian war of 1962, already understood the strategic interest of a rapprochement with China which it tried to use to its advantage on the occasion of its war against India in 1965. Nevertheless one had to wait for the year 1971 to see Nixon and Kissinger drawing the full implication of the Sino-Soviet split for the USA. This happened during the Bangladesh crisis when a new USA-China axis emerged, opening a new phase in the Cold War era.

The British Balanced View over the Bangladesh Crisis

The study of the FO archives concerning the Bangladesh war shows two main points, which do not correspond fully with the impression one could get through the reading of the press reports of the time. Firstly, London did not really subscribe to the American view of the conflict. Secondly, London was more struck by the moderation of the main actors engaged in the conflict than by the risk of an extension of the conflict.

Informing the FCO about Indira Gandhi's conversations with the American leaders during her visit to the USA in November 1971, the UK Ambassador in Washington wrote: 'In all talks, Americans had been at pains to dispel any impression that they were approaching the situation in one-sided manner.'[105] Obviously, the British diplomacy was adopting a much more balanced attitude. To understand these divergent approaches, the fact that London and Washington did not perform the same function in the world has to be considered. London, as an observer and a junior partner in the Western camp, was bound to focus its attention on the regional aspect of the conflict. Washington, as the leading country of the Western bloc, kept an eye on its global dimensions. This phenomenon comes out clearly in a record of a December 1971 discussion between the Foreign and Commonwealth Secretary, Alec Douglas Home and the Assistant to the US President for National Security Affairs, Henry Kissinger:

Kissinger did not accept our differences over the India/Pakistan conflict were a matter of different assessments. The President [Nixon]'s concern had never been purely with the local situation; indeed since March the American government, like the British government had accepted that East Pakistan would become independent, sooner or later. Their [America's] policy had been to bring it about peacefully and if possible by agreement. Their major concern however had been to ensure that the Russians should not conclude that they could stir up trouble anywhere, even somewhere so out of the way and divorced from direct US interests as the Indian sub-continent, without evoking an American response. The Soviet Union might not have actually provoked the Indians into going to war but they had done nothing to restrain them.[106]

In fact, London's diplomatic establishment did not share Kissinger's and Nixon's strong anti-Indian feelings. 'We hear', wrote the British, 'a great deal in White House circles about the shiftiness and hypocrisy of the Indians. Mr. Nixon seems instinctively to see the Pakistanis as the honest "hard cats" of the region—good friends to have in a tight corner, ham-handed perhaps but thoroughly honest. The Indians in contrast are self-seeking, dishonest and above all moralistic—a version in short of Lord Macauley's "wily Hindu" thesis.'[107] Kissinger, London remarked, even went to the extent of thinking that the 'guerilla sorties', and the 'artillery harassment' the Indian authorities organized at the border between East and West Bengal, were 'one deliberate deterrent to the refugees [East Pakistanis] returning'.[108]

British diplomats clearly did not appreciate very much the personal role of Kissinger whose behaviour did not follow traditional diplomatic patterns. Their dispatches contained a thinly veiled criticism upon the 'considerations of Macht Politik' which 'are always in the forefront of Kissinger's thoughts'.[109] They dissociated themselves from 'the emotional factor' they discerned in Kissinger's fascination for China, 'from which even officials do not appear immune'. The American visit to the Great Wall did not impress them: '[It is] really disheartening to see the cream of the National Security bureaucracy being paraded for photographs with Chou, entirely to suit his book, like a troop of floppy trousered Albanians' [110] They did not fail to notice that Kissinger 'left all his shirts in Islamabad' when he left for China from Pakistan and described it as a 'beautiful symbolism'. Neither did they fail to report that, once in China, 'on two occasions Kissinger left the famous book of instructions behind in the guest house, to the consternation of his staff'.[111]

London did not believe either that India wanted to attack West Pakistan. True, the British documents indicate no sign of basic sympathy towards India. Not a single dispatch, not a single report underlined one of the fundamental ingredients of the Bangladesh war: West Pakistan's refusal to accept the results of the democratic legislative elections of 1970. During her tour in Europe, the Indian Prime Minister Indira Gandhi went on repeating that the Bangladesh situation had been created by Pakistan itself.[112] She obviously failed to convince her interlocutors. But London did not adopt an openly pro-Pakistan's stand. In particular, London did not give much credit to the Americans when they said that India might attack West Pakistan. At the peak of the Indo-Pakistan tension in December 1971, Kissinger informed the UK Ambassador in Washington about the existence of an aide-mémoire given to Ayub Khan in 1962 by the then US Ambassador in Pakistan, reaffirming that the US government 'will come to Pakistan's assistance in the event of aggression from India'.[113] Kissinger also said that according to 'some American intelligence sources', Indira Gandhi had the 'intention to destroy the Pakistan army to facilitate definitive acquisition of Kashmir'. He explained the sending of the aircraft carrier *Enterprise* to the Indian Ocean in these terms: 'American policy is aimed at searing off Indian attack on West Pakistan. America cannot afford to give appearance of caving in against situation where Russian military and political support is as overt as it is in India. This would greatly weaken American influence in Middle East and other trouble spots.'[114] British archives show that the British did not take for granted the information given to them by Kissinger and that they had serious doubt about its veracity. On 18 December 1971, the South Asian Department was categorical: 'It is not, we believe, an Indian aim to destroy West Pakistan and we do not share American fears on this account.'[115] In fact, even if the Bangladesh events were taken as a crisis, it does not appear that the UK government ever really expected it to develop into a global war or even into a larger confrontation. Moderation was the keyword used generally by London to qualify the Indian policy in 1971. Many factors explained the British perception.

First of all, there was the personality of Indira Gandhi. The Indian Prime Minister was perceived as a strong leader whose policy constituted a 'personal affront' to President Nixon.[116] British believed that she did not favour a dialogue with Pakistan and its leader Yahya Khan and she even thought that if Mujibur Rahman were to adopt a conciliatory approach with the Pakistani dictator, the East Pakistan people would no longer recognize him as their leader in the struggle for liberation.[117] But at the same time, whatever her 'intellectual and emotional leaning towards Moscow',[118] her 'left-wing views are more doctrinaire rather than intellectual' and 'India's drift towards the Soviet Union did not indicate her wish to cut India's ties with the West. She might have reservations about the Soviet Union's long term intentions.'[119] In other words, 'Mrs Gandhi is likely to be aware that Russians motives are not altruistic.'[120] The British Prime Minister himself in a cabinet meeting stressed that Indira Gandhi told him she was under the pressure of hawks in her own cabinet and that she was somehow prepared not to submit to their views.[121] On a more global level, the Indian attitude towards Western military presence in Asia was perceived by the British not as anti-West, but as 'ambivalent': 'While they [the Indians] would like to see American forces leave South East Asia, they would equally like to know they are available just over the horizon.'[122]

Second, London had been convinced by A.K. Damodaran, Minister in the Indian Embassy in Moscow, and T.N. Kaul, the Foreign Secretary, that the Indo-Soviet treaty of August 1971 did not constitute an aggressive treaty against the West. Damodaran told the British that

> [its] genesis goes back to 1968 when the Soviet Union was supplying arms to Pakistan and this led to Indian protests. The Russian had then tried to reassure the Indians with the arguments that if they did not show friendship to Pakistan in this way it would leave the field open for the penetration of Chinese influence which could not be to India's benefit. The Indians had not been impressed by the argument and the Russians, in order to reinforce such assurances, had offered the Indians a treaty.[123]

According to Damodaran, the Congress split of 1969 and its political consequences had made the offer to come to nothing, even if the treaty had existed in a draft form since 1969. T.N. Kaul confirmed this story, underlining 'that the concept of a treaty had been under discussion for five and a half to six years'. 'There is no reason to doubt this', said the British Foreign and Commonwealth Office.[124]

Thirdly, under these circumstances, London saw even some reasons to consider the Indo-Soviet treaty as something positive. The treaty was analysed as a way for the Soviet Union to put some pressure to restrain India. For this reason, 'to the extent that the treaty lessens the war, and for the moment at least it would seem to, it must I think be welcomed', the UKHC in Delhi wrote.[125] The UK Ambassador in Washington expressed the same opinion, adding that Russia might consider the treaty as a way to make India more moderate: 'The reason why the Russians had chosen to agree now were probably various.

China was a factor. But the most pressing reason was no doubt fear that Mrs Gandhi was on the point of announcing recognition of Bangladesh. . . . The Russians presumably hoped with the treaty to have purchased some measure of control over Indian actions vis-à-vis Pakistan.'[126] The Pakistan Ambassador in the USSR sang the same refrain to his British colleague in Moscow: '[His] impression is that the Russians are generally anxious to prevent any further worsening of the situation and are genuinely afraid that only the Chinese would profit from this.'[127] The UK Embassy in Moscow confirmed this perception: 'The Russians [are] actively encouraging the Indian government to continue this "moderate" policy.' The dispatch even insisted: 'Damodaran said that the Soviet government was apprehensive about the growth of chaotic conditions in East Pakistan; they saw it is a potential threat to their interests and something that could only benefit the Chinese. He was convinced that the Russians would continue to be very cautious in their attitude to East Pakistan separatism.'[128] A report written on Prime Minister's demand and submitted to the Cabinet on the 'likely course of events and consequences' of an extension of the Bangladesh crisis even stated that Moscow might not respect the treaty in case of a war between India and West Pakistan:

> We do not think it likely that any great power could intervene militarily in the subcontinent. The Soviet Union has shown themselves anxious to prevent any Indo-Pakistan conflict and through they may now be becoming more resigned to the possibility, we do not think that they would regard themselves as bound under the Indo-Soviet treaty to come to India's aid militarily even if it were immediately clear that Pakistan had started hostilities.[129]

Fourthly, London did not believe that the Sino-Indian relations were as bad as to engender a war between these two countries. Indira Gandhi herself told the FC secretary that 'it was her impression that in the present crisis China had been far less provocative than in 1965. As soon as they had realised how seriously the East Bengalis were fighting, the Chinese had moderated their overt support for Yahya.'[130] Analysing the 'political relations between India and China', the UKHC in Delhi distinguished two Indian 'schools of thought'. The first one thought that India had done enough to indicate to China that it wanted to have better relations with Beijing (the Director of the East Asia Division of the South Block, V.V. Paranjpe, was said to belong to this 'school'). The second one would have liked to use the result of the 1971 legislative election—excellent for Indira Gandhi—to develop better relations with China in the hope of dissociating Beijing from Islamabad.[131] The fact that British diplomats analysed Bhutto's visit to China as a failure for Pakistan confirmed their own conviction that China had no real intention to intervene militarily in the conflict.[132] Some Indian diplomats also told the British that they thought China would not endanger its rapprochement with the USA, following Kissinger's visit, by launching a war against India. The only leader who seemed to have feared a war between India and China was Kissinger who told the British Ambassador in Washington in July 1971, 'that he was deeply disturbed about the likelihood of the outbreak of war between India and Pakistan and if this were to occur he thought it only too probable that the Chinese would fully support the Pakistanis. This would escalate the confrontation in a most dangerous way.'[133] And, one may add, this would have singularly jeopardized the Sino-American rapprochement so well secretly prepared by Kissinger and Nixon.

Fifthly and last, the prospect of an independent Bangladesh under the political influence of India did not frighten the British. India, they thought, would do her best to check the Maoist threat in this part of the world. Of course, London was afraid that in the long run the Indians would not 'take seriously . . . the much more insidious . . . endeavour of the Soviet Union to secure a grip on their system from within'. In several cases, the UKHC in Delhi wrote, 'their psychological defence against Russian penetration have been undermined'. But the UKHC, who had been posted in Delhi at the turn of the 1950s, reassured himself with the idea that Indian diplomats were more realistic than they were before: 'Both in Delhi and elsewhere', he commented emphatically, 'most Indian diplomats have left Olympus and rejoined the human race. Their perspective has, for the most part, contracted and they interest themselves mainly in countries and issues that are of direct concern to India: Africa has, for example, shrunk from their horizon. Stripped of their halos, their opportunism show through, but at least their feet are generally closer to the ground.'[134] In other words, India would be now more conscious of its immediate national interest. The British perception was that the Bangladesh episode might well open a new transition area for the Indian foreign policy, a little more away from its Nehruvian legacy.

Notes

1. United Kingdom High Commissioner (UKHC) in India to the CRO, 27 February 1958. FO 371/135947.
2. Letter of the UKHC in India to the CRO, 29 August 1952. FL 1022/9.

3. FO comment (W.B. Ledwige) on a dispatch from the UKHC in India, 30 July 1948, F 11837/76/85.
4. Letter of the UKHC in India to the CRO, 29 August 1952, FL 1022/9.
5. FO note, 13 November 1948, F 16460/6/65.
6. Note of the UKHC in India to the CRO, December 1953, FY 1192/102.
7. Dispatch, 17 March 1951, FL 10345/3.
8. C. Auchinleck to Wavell, 11 May 1946. Quoted in M.N. Das, *Partition and Independence of India: Inside Story of the Mountbatten Days*, New Delhi: Vision Books, 1982, p. 266.
9. 'The Russian menace to India', 3 December 1947, F 15955/8800/85.
10. 'Probable effects of a Pakistan contribution to Middle East defence', note of the UKHC in Delhi to the CRO, 13 November 1951, FO 371/101134.
11. Letter of the UKHC in India to the CRO, 30 January 1952, FL 1022/1.
12. Ibid.
13. Anthony Eden, *The Memoirs of Sir Anthony Eden*, London: Full Circle, 1960, p. 97.
14. 'Attitude of the Government of India to colonial affairs', Joint Memorandum (draft) by the Secretaries of State for the Colonies and Commonwealth Relations, n.d., *c.* May 1954, DL 1061/15.
15. Letter of the UKHC in India to the FO, 5 August 1950, FK 1022/27b.
16. Letter of the UKHC in India to the CRO, 21 June 1949, F 9836:1026/85g.
17. Comment on a letter of the UKHC in India to the FO, 25 August 1951, FL 10345/8.
18. Anthony Eden, *Mémoires. L'épreuve de force, février 1938-août 1954*, Paris: Plon, p. 402.
19. India decided to remain in the Commonwealth in May 1949. FO comment of a CRO report, February 1948, F 5793/76/85g.
20. Note from a businessman to the CRO, 28 November 1953, FO 371/106861.
21. Note of the CRO (South East Asian Department) on the US-UK economic relations, 27 May 1954, FO 371/112217.
22. CRO dispatch to the UKHC in India, 28 November 1953, FL 1192/1.
23. UKHC in India dispatch to the CRO, 2 January 1954, DY 1192/7 (a).
24. These are the words of the UKHC in Pakistan, quoted in a confidential report of the CRO ('United States military aid to Pakistan'), 2 January 1953, DY 1192/16.
25. Note of the FO ('The Russian menace to India'), 3 December 1947, F 15955/8800/85.
26. 'The Inter-Asian Relations Conference', report of the Royal Institute of International Affairs, 16 April 1947, F 5989/919/61.
27. 6 December 1950, FL 1017:18.
28. Dispatch of the UK Embassy in Moscow, 6 January 1948, F 637/49/85.
29. Dispatch, 23 March 1950, FT 1068/3.
30. Dispatch, 6 September 1950. FT 1061/8.

31. Dispatch, 17 August 1950, FT 1061/6.
32. According a dispatch of the UKHC in India to the CRO, 6 September 1950, FT 1061/8.
33. Letter of the UKHC in India to the CRO, 29 August 1952, FL 1022/9.
34. Letter of Nehru to Panikkar, 25 October 1950. Quoted in S. Gopal, *Jawaharlal Nehru: A Biography*, vol. 2, London: Jonathan Cape, 1979, pp.107-8.
35. Dispatch of the CRO on a conversation between Zhou Enlai and K.M. Panikkar in Beijing, 14 December 1950, KK 1042/8.
36. Letter of the UKHC in India to the CRO, 29 August 1952, FL 1022/9.
37. 'The Inter-Asian Relations Conference', report of the Royal Institute of International Affairs, 16 April 1947, F 5989/919/61.
38. Letter of the UKHC in India to the CRO, 30 January 1952, FL 1022/1.
39. FO (Far East Section) comment to a CRO's report, 20 February 1948, F 5793/76/85g.
40. Note of the UKHC in India to the FO, 6 September 1949, F 14624/1022/82.
41. FO note, 1948, F 146114/6/85.
42. Letter of the UKHC in India to the CRO, 3 June 1953, FL 1018/1.
43. Note of the FO (preparing Mountbatten's visit to India), 26 November 1947, F 15639/8800/85.
44. See Letter of the Secretary of State for Commonwealth Relations to the Defence Minister, 14 June 1948, and annexed file, F 1864c/76/85/g.
45. Note of the UKHC in India to the Cabinet Office, 28 March 1947, F 4378/919/61.
46. Report of the UKHC in India to the CRO on 'A review of Communist activities in India', 20 May 1953, FL 1016/3.
47. Ton That Thien, *India and South East Asia: 1947-1960*, Geneva: Droz, 1963, p. 107.
48. FO minutes, 10 July 1950, FH 1064/8.
49. Letter of the UKHC in India to the CRO, 30 January 1952, FL 1022/1.
50. Anthony Eden, *The Memoirs of Sir Anthony Eden*, op. cit., pp. 123-4.
51. Letter of the UKHC in India to the CRO, 8 February 1952, FN 10385/4.
52. Letter of the UKHC in India to the CRO, 28 August 1952, FL 1022/9.
53. 'India's North-East Frontier Policy', FO Research Department, 2 June 1954, para. 22, DL/1022/2.
54. Note of the UK ambassador in Beijing, 4 April 1954, F 1072/3.
55. Sources of the quotations: Letter of the UKHC in India ('Probable effects of a Pakistan contribution to Middle East Defence') to Sir Percival Liesching, CRO, 13 November 1951, and letter of the UKHC in Pakistan to Sir Percival Liesching, CRO, 8 November 1951, FO 371/10134.
56. Memorandum of a discussion between Nehru and the British Finance Minister, 2 February 1955, DL 1022/2.

57. Dispatch of the UK Embassy in Washington, 12 January 1956, DL/10338/5.
58. Dispatch of the UK Embassy in Moscow, 27 February 1962, NS 1022/18.
59. Dispatch of the UK Embassy in Washington, 12 January 1956, DL 10338/5.
60. Dispatch of the UKHC in Pakistan, 6 March 1956, DL 10338/11. See also discussion between Nehru, UKHC in India, Lord Mountbatten and N.R. Pillai, 17 March 1956, DL 10338/13.
61. Words of the American ambassador to the UKHC in Pakistan, dispatch of 4 December 1953, FY 1192/91.
62. 'Now that the Soviet government finds it expedient to show friendly face to the Indian . . .', Dispatch of the British Embassy in Moscow to the FO, 14 February 1955, NS 10385/6.
63. Note of the FO (Northern Department), 13 August 1959, NS 10345/105.
64. Note of the FO (Northern Department), 6 October 1959, NS 10345/47.
65. Note of the UK Embassy in China, 4 February 1953, FL 10310/1.
66. Note of the UK Embassy in China, 11 March 1953, FL 10310/2.
67. Dispatch of the UK Embassy in Moscow, 4 December 1953, FY 1192/61.
68. Note to the CRO, 21 November 1953, DL 10338/1.
69. Dispatch of the UK Embassy in China, 16 December 1953, FC 1903/4.
70. Ibid.
71. Letter of the UKHC in India to the CRO, 9 June 1954, DL 1022/13.
72. Dispatch of the UK Ambassador in China, discussed in the FO, 16 August 1954, FC 1024/46.
73. Ibid.
74. Letter of the UK Ambassador in China, November 1954, FC 10385/30.
75. FO note, 25 February 1955, NS 10310/2.
76. Khrushchev underlined to a GDR delegation in Moscow, dispatch of 17 September 1955, FC 1021/16.
77. Note of the UK Ambassador in China, 23 December 1954, FC 10385/1.
78. Note of the UK Ambassador in Moscow, 4 May 1956, FC 10338/10.
79. Note of the UKHC in India, 11 September 1956, DL 10310/5.
80. Said the Prime Secretary of the Indian Embassy in China. Dispatch of the UK Ambassador in China, 12 September 1959, FC 1091/22.
81. Dispatch of the UK Ambassador in India, 21 October 1959, FC 1091/53.
82. Dispatch of the UK Ambassador in India, 13 July 1960, FC 1091/45.
83. Dispatch of the UK Ambassador in India, 27 May 1960, DL 1022/7.
84. Dispatch of the UKHC in India, 10 November 1959, FC 1091/64.
85. Conversation between Radhakrishnan and McDonald, London, 2 April 1960, FC 1091/26.
86. Dispatch of the UKHC in India, 27 April 1960, FC 1091/29.
87. FO note, 9 January 1960, FC 1091/7.

88. Dispatch of the UKHC in India, 13 July 1960, FC 1091/45.
89. Said the Indian Ambassador in UK, London, 2 November 1962, FC 1061/142.
90. FO minutes, 20 November 1962, FC 1061/254.
91. Pillai told: 'public opinion would not accept any concessions' (dispatch of the UKHC in India, 27 April 1960, FC 1091/29). He added, 'The state of feeling in India was such that not even Mr Nehru could have got away publicly with concessions in Ladakh in return for the recognition of the McMahon line' (CRO note, 28 April 1960, FC 1091/32). The Joint Secretary of South Block said: 'public opinion and Parliament could not allowed him [Nehru] to make concessions' (conversation between C.M. Anderson and K.L. Mehta, 4 May 1960, FC 1091/34). Krishna Menon declared, 'he [Nehru] was forced to deny it [an agreement with China] by the strength of his compatriot's present opinion to any such deal' (dispatch of the UKHC in India, 13 July 1960, FC 1091/45). Morarji Desai stated, 'the Indian parliamentary and public opinion would not permit it and if Nehru tried to cede territory to China, he would be put out of office as Prime Minister' (dispatch of the UKHC in India, 5 April 1960, DL 10310/14). In November 1962, Pillai said that a concession 'was no longer possible for domestic political reasons' (FO note, 2 November 1962, FC 1061/142). In April 1960, Vice-President Radhakrishnan considered that Nehru's public declaration 'now makes it impossible for him to make any substantial concession to meet the Chinese. He said that Mr Nehru's statements had united the whole Indian people behind the government against any surrender of territory and he seemed to imply that Mr Nehru should have left himself at least a little room for manoeuvre' (conversation between Radhakrishnan and McDonald, London, 2 April 1960, FC 1991/26).
92. These are K.L. Mehta 'personal observations' conveyed to the British, note of the UKHC in India, 4 May 1960, FC 1091/34.
93. Dispatch of the UKHC in India, 21 October 1959, FC 1091/53.
94. CRO note, 28 April 1960, FC 1091/32.
95. Dispatch of the UK Ambassador in Moscow, 11 July 1962, FC 1061/46.
96. FO comment on a note of the UK Chargé d'Affaires in China, 30 June 1962, FC 1061/45.
97. Dispatch of the UKHC in India, 24 October 1962, FC 1061/106.
98. Ibid. Dispatch of the UKHC in India, 21 October 1959, FC 1091/53.
99. 'Soviet policy towards India, as well as Soviet handling of the Cuban episode, have recently exacerbated Sino-Soviet relations, already bad, to a point of extreme bitterness. Unless Khrushchev is willing to risk an open break (which seems unlikely) this is another reason for thinking that he will not be interested in any substantial measures to improve East-West relations. Such measures would involve him in real concessions on basic issues and could be presented against him as negotiation from weakness.' Brief, NATO ministerial meeting, Paris, 13-15 December 1963, NS 12022/96.

100. Dispatch of the UKHC in India, 24 October 1962, FC 1061/106.
101. Dispatch of the UKHC in India, 3 November 1959, FC 1091/62.
102. In 1957, the FO already envisaged the possibility to attract China towards the West: 'It seems at least fairly certain that in the near future, at any rate, if we do not give China a chance to associate with the West she will be driven more and more to tie herself to the Soviet Union' (FC 10338/10). This 'chance' was conceived as a way to limit the prospect of a close Sino-Soviet cooperation. After the Sino-Soviet split, the Western camp would hope to draw China towards the West against the Soviet Union.
103. Dispatch of the UKHC in Pakistan, 28 October 1959, FC 1081/3.
104. Note of the UK Ambassador in Moscow, 27 February 1962, NS 1022/18.
105. Dispatch of the UK Ambassador in USA to the Foreign and Commonwealth Office, 9 November 1971, FCO 37/827.
106. Record of a conversation between the Foreign and Commonwealth Secretary and H. Kissinger, 20 December 1971, FCO 37/754.
107. Note of the UK Ambassador in Washington ('US policy towards the subcontinent'), 10 December 1971, FCO 37/755.
108. Telegram of the UK Ambassador in Washington ('Kissinger's visit to India and Pakistan'), 21 July 1971, FCO 21/828.
109. Note of the UK Ambassador in Washington, 10 December 1971, FCO 37/755.
110. Dispatch of the UK Embassy in Washington to the FCO (Far Eastern Department), 19 November 1971, FCO 21/827.
111. Dispatch of the UK Embassy in Washington to the FCO (Far Eastern Department), 17 August 1971, FCO 21/827.
112. 'Visit of Mrs Gandhi, Indian Prime Minister, to UK, 29 October to 31 October 1971', FCO 37/825 and /826.
113. Dispatch of the UK Ambassador in Washington to the FCO, 12 December 1971, Cabinet documents, PREM 15.571
114. Ibid.
115. Note of the South Asian Department, 18 December 1971, FCO 37/756.
116. Note of the UK Ambassador in Washington ('US policy towards the subcontinent'), 10 December 1971, FCO 37/755.
117. Record of a conversation between the FC Secretary and Mrs. Gandhi, 1 November 1971, FCO 37/826.
118. Letter of the UKHC in India to the FC Secretary of State, 9 January 1970, FCO 37/371.
119. Biographical note on Mrs. Gandhi, 21 October 1971, FCO 37/826.
120. UKHC in India, report on 'The Indo-Soviet treaty: what price non-alignment?', August 1971, FCO 37/819.
121. Record of a meeting between E. Hearth and Indira Gandhi, 31 October 1971, Cabinet Documents, PREM 15-569.

122. FCO comment on a letter from the UKHC in India, 9 January 1970, FCO 37/371.
123. Note of the UK Embassy in Moscow, 9 November 1971, FCO 37/816.
124. UKHC in India, report on 'The Indo-Soviet treaty: what price non-alignment?', August 1971, FCO 37/819.
125. Ibid.
126. Letter of the UK Ambassador in Washington, 12 August 1971, FCO 37/819.
127. Letter of the UK Ambassador in Moscow to the FCO, 3 July 1971, FCO 37/927.
128. Letter of the UK Ambassador in Moscow to the FCO, 26 April 1971.
129. Cabinet documents, CAB. 130/542.
130. Record of a discussion between the FC Secretary and Indira Gandhi, 1 November 1971, FCO 37/826.
131. Note of the UKHC in India, 8 April 1971, FCO 37/818.
132. FCO note ('Political relations between Pakistan and China'), November 1971, FCO 37/903.
133. Telegram from the UK Ambassador in Washington, 21 July 1971, FCO 21/828.
134. Letter of the UKHC in India ('Indian foreign policy'), 9 January 1970, FCO 37/371.

MAX-JEAN ZINS

❖ The Chinese Factor in the American Policy towards India: Some Clues from the US Archives

Analysing the American perception of India's foreign policy in view of the Chinese factor is indeed an ambitious exercise. China always played a role in the US policy towards India. Two drastically different periods can be distinguished since India's Independence in 1947 and since the Chinese Revolution of 1949. In the first one, China was the main enemy of the United States in Asia, as it was the largest country allied to the Soviet Union. Americans felt that India could be used to minimize the Chinese influence in Asia. As a non-aligned country strongly attached to its national independence, India could not be coerced to play an active role against China in the East-West confrontation. Nevertheless, it presented the convincing image of a democratic counter-model to Communist China. Even if Washington was often irritated by India's external policy and, hence, decided to rely on Pakistan—the arch enemy of India—to contain communism in this part of the world, India kept a reasonably favourable image in the American perception vis-à-vis the abhorred China. Washington took a decade or so to understand the benefit it could draw from the division of the communist world into two antagonist poles around Moscow and Beijing at the end of the 1950s. Then, the second period began with the secret visit of the adviser to US President Richard Nixon, Henry Kissinger, to China in 1971. This visit and its consequence—the rapid improvement of the Sino-American relations—represented one of the most important diplomatic initiatives of the Cold War, as China became a new tacit ally of Washington against Soviet Union. It had an immediate impact on the Indo-American relations which India realized during the Bangladesh crisis when its importance decreased in American eyes. For Washington, Delhi's external policy tended to appear merely as an extension of the foreign policy of Soviet Union. It is in the frame of these drastic changes that I will study how the Indian diplomacy tried to answer the challenges that the American policy presented for it. The American archives will provide some clues to this.

BEFORE 1971: THE IMPORTANCE OF BEING INDIA

Washington started paying attention to India even before 1947, viewing it with a measure of sympathy. The American leaders were attracted by the idea of a united India with its immense mineral resources and expressed their interest by supporting the cause of independence. However, in practice, their alliance with the UK during the Second World War led them not to antagonize Churchill on this issue, an issue which was at the root of the first important Indo-US divergence. In 1947, South Asia was not a priority for American diplomacy as much as Europe obviously was. It did not mean that Americans were unaware of India—in fact, the archives show that they knew much more than is generally considered— but it did not figure high in their priorities. One of the reasons for this relative non-interest lay in the fact that they did not seem overly afraid of a Communist threat to India. True, their first Ambassador in New Delhi, Henry Grady, wrote to Washington (November 1947): 'We do not want, I am sure, India to become another Greece.'[1] But Washington appeared to be finally more worried about the 'balkanization' or 'fragmentation' of India than by Communism casting a shadow over the government. For example, in 1947, 'a separatist move of Hyderabad' was seen as a possible 'prelude to a fragmentation process which might have far reaching effects on any plan for ultimate Indian unity'.[2] The American envoy, knowing that 'there is a danger of Hyderabad trying to use its trade representation as a entering wedge', alerted the State Department's Division of South Asian Affairs, cautioning that 'it will have to be watched constantly'.[3] Whereas the US Embassy in Delhi, contradicting a report of John Foster Dulles, wrote impassively that it 'has observed no indication of Soviet influence on interim government. Most individuals in government which is primarily representative of propertied and conservative classes seem rather to fear communist infiltration. . . . Congress has been making strenuous efforts during [the] past year to counteract communist activities.'[4]

Notwithstanding articles in the Indian print media or public political statements, the tone of Indian diplomatic discourse with the Americans was quite clear. Both the Secretary-General of the Ministry of External Affairs, Girija Shankar Bajpai, and the Indian Ambassador in Washington, Asaf Ali, pointed out the need to develop India as a non-communist entity in South Asia. For instance, Asaf Ali stated in 1947 that 'if India becomes strong it would be a bastion for the world against the great northern neighbour which now casts its shadow over two continents. To the left and right flank of India the countries were weak but India might servc as a strong center between weaker neighbours.'[5] In fact, after Independence, Indian and Pakistani diplomats seemed to compete in trying to convince America that they have to be supported against an eventual communist menace. Bajpai in 1948 said in Washington: 'India can expect no effective assistance from the USSR in its primary objective of developing and strengthening itself economically and militarily. In fact, the US is the only country which is in a position to aid India'.[6] Even Sheikh Abdullah, leader of the National Conference of Kashmir, presented its claim for an independent Kashmir in these terms in 1948: 'it would be much better if Kashmir were independent and would seek American and British aid for development'.[7] All this could not but provide a sense of relief to the Americans, who sometimes seemed to think that Pakistan would indeed be more threatened by communism than India.

Nor did Washington see a strong and immediate menace from the USSR for the subcontinent. According to the Office of South Asian Affairs in 1950, 'Communism does not immediately threatens the governments of South Asia. The USSR is not exerting in this region the direct pressure evident in Iran and Indochina.'[8] Moreover, Americans—at least some of them—perceived China to be so weak that it could not represent a real challenge for the region in 1949-50. The US Ambassador to the UN believed thus a few days after the proclamation of the People's Republic of China that 'no government could live in China without external assistance and support'.[9]

Under these circumstances, Washington felt no need to divert much of its financial and military resources to aid India. In 1948, Bajpai was frankly told by Loy Henderson, the Director of the Office of Near Eastern and African Affairs and who was to become the next US Ambassador to India, that 'unfortunately at the moment the United States finds it necessary the concentrate its efforts and resources on resisting aggression in certain other parts of the world', and that India will be given 'proper and essential attention . . . just as soon as circumstances permitted'.[10] In 1950, Henderson clearly stated 'that regardless of what India's foreign policy might be it should not expect any substantial quantities of arms from US in near future'.[11] Consciously,

Washington decided to keep a rather low profile in South Asia. In 1948, the Under Secretary of State, Robert Lovett, went to the extent of recommending a cautious behaviour on the Kashmir issue for the reason stating that any 'marked initiative by the United States in this dispute might attract undesirable Russian attention'.[12]

The Korean war was a landmark for the USA and, in a sense, the watershed of their new policy towards South Asia. According to the Director of the Near Eastern, South Asian and African Affairs, George McGhee: 'The Korean War may well mean that the struggle of the USSR and the free world has been transferred to Asia. . . . The Chinese Communists might move next in extended aggression to the South Asian areas. The South Asian countries, in particular India and Pakistan, represent a nucleus of strength.'[13] He added that 'with the crisis in Korea . . . our policy has become somewhat more positive and we have taken an increased interest in their military strength'.[14] There is also an expressed intent to intervene on the economic front: 'all are expose to communist pressure. . . . Experience has shown that countries in such proximity to the USSR orbit need the stiffening and confidence provided by the United States economic assistance.'[15] In this apparently new US frame of mind, India—and Pakistan for the same reason—suddenly acquired a new importance for Washington. And of course China, whose activism had to be watched carefully.

Originally, India seemed to appear relatively more important than Pakistan for Washington. 'It was clear that in the last analysis Asia could be rid of communism only by Asian themselves and it was to our best interest to build our hopes on India', McGhee said in 1950.[16] India's natural resources are often cited when endorsing closer relations which are said to be 'most useful to our national defence'.[17] By contrast, Pakistan's resources were obviously less significant, the country being essentially 'a potentially efficient agricultural producer and exporter' which 'might play a key role in our economic policy for South and East Asia, provided continued differences with India do not disrupt the Pakistan economy'.[18] The problem for America was that India, totally determined to keep an independent path, did not want to join the Western bloc and did not share the American analysis of the Communist threat. Pakistan would in time become the military ally of America and the 'free world' in the region. Politically and perceptibly the process started as early as 1951.

India, in any case, was perceived as a moderate country that did not intend to join the Communist bloc. Like Pakistan, it had a 'free middle-of-the-road government'.[19] Internally, 'the government has taken vigorous and reasonably effective steps to limit [Communist Party of India] activities and influence'.[20] Externally, notably in South-East Asia, Nehru adopted a policy which 'served our interest admirably'.[21] This moderation made Washington presciently expect that India would not associate itself with the Eastern bloc even if its Pakistan enemy entered into a military alliance with the West. It also allowed Washington not to offer much help for Indian defence in view of the American shortages in this respect in the early 1950s.[22]

India did not share America's approach to the China question though. For its own reasons (Taiwan, Korea, etc.) Washington adopted a line of direct confrontation with Communist China, including the refusal to establish diplomatic relations with Beijing. In particular, the 'containment of Communism' strategy implied a refusal to deduce any significant difference between USSR and China. Both countries were considered strong allies and closely connected. India's stand was different. It is often argued that Nehru's policy towards China was unrealistic, somehow utopian, and was based on a faulty assessment of real Chinese strength and intent. Notwithstanding the conventional opinion on Nehru, an examination of the American archives may lead to different conclusions. Obviously, for Nehru, Communist China represented 'a problematical neighbour'.[23] In 1951, conversing with Chester Bowles, US Ambassador to India, he insisted that he was not 'in any way blind to potential dangers which might be developing in India'. Joking about his own Ambassador to China, K.M. Panikkar, who 'usually succumbed to whatever situation he was in', Nehru said categorically that he did not accept 'Panikkar's present views about China'.[24] In fact, Nehru believed that 'the spirit of aggressiveness' he found in China was not a mere consequence of Communist proselytism, but also due to a 'virile' desire of expressing strong nationalist feelings.[25] It is in this framework that one must understand the anxious attention Nehru paid to China's ability to implement agrarian reforms and conversely his awareness of the agrarian weakness of India. He understood quite well the implications of Chinese economic gains which, he said, 'might considerably exceed those of India' in the next few years. The Chinese 'vitality' that he spoke of more than once to the American diplomats and leaders obviously represented a challenge to the Indian leader. Because of the potential danger he perceived, Nehru resorted to certain colonial stereotypes while rationalizing that 'China has taken much better care of her soil' while 'Indians living in hotter climate less able take long hours in fields which Chinese endure with relative ease'.[26] He acknowledged 'that it is quite possible the new China would develop into explosive dangerous force and that in this case US would appear to have been right'.[27] Knowing that 'two thousand miles frontier between India and communist country could not be ignored', Nehru suggested that the Americans should follow a more subtle strategy vis-à-vis China.[28] The Indian prime minister did not want to consolidate China in its international isolation, an attitude that could only either increase the risk of a war or lead Beijing to strengthen its ties with Moscow. He explained that 'there was no essential difference between his approach and that other free nations except as to method', the American Ambassador wrote in a dispatch.[29]

From this arose one of the main US-India divergences; Washington did not want to see any difference between Moscow and Beijing, whereas Nehru tried to convince the Americans that they were wrong. As early as 1948, Nehru insisted 'that a communist China would not necessarily [be] dominated by Soviet Union'.[30] The American Ambassador noted down that C. Rajagopalachari, the then Governor General, 'went so far as to say that China under communist control would probably [be] more Asiatic and anti-Western and might therefore be more co-operative with India than Kuomintang China. . . .'[31] In 1949, Nehru told President Truman, that Russia 'could not [for] long dominate China', foreseeing that a situation 'stronger than a Titoism' would grow up.'[32] He reaffirmed in 1951 that 'he [is] sure it [China] would eventually disentangle itself from Russia although process might be many years duration'.[33] 'It was the Prime Minister's opinion that the objective should be to divert the [Chinese] Communists away from Moscow leadership as quickly as possible', reported the Americans in 1949.[34] They noted again in 1951 that 'he earnestly believed . . . [that the] best hope was an attempt to divide Russia and China'.[35]

A Counter Model not a Counterweight

In the mid-1950s, a new epoch emerged in the subcontinent. Firstly, Pakistan was firmly linked to the Western camp while India had to cope with this unpleasant reality. In a way, this confirmed the conclusion of a CIA memorandum of 1951 which stated that India was against a militant attitude towards China, 'because of a desire to get along with a powerful neighbour, particularly as long as India is militarily preoccupied with Pakistan'.[36] Secondly, USSR was becoming an important economic and diplomatic actor in South Asia, by making India its primary target for getting a foothold into to the non-Communist developing world. Thirdly, China was developing more rapidly than India and was now able to play an important role not only in Asia but also in the world at large. For the National Security Council Planning Board, 'the rapid growth in Chinese communist power . . . underlines the desirability of developing in India a successful alternative to communism in an Asiatic context'.[37] It is this expectation that was of particular relevance, one that had political, economic and diplomatic implications.

In the economic field, raising India as an alternative to China compelled the US to spend more money on India than ever before. Economic assistance became the keyword in the Indo-American relationship. Consequently, a whole new series of problems and issues with their own specificity, contradictions, and ramifications, arose between Washington and Delhi.[38] Politically, a new emphasis was put on India as a 'model of democracy'. As the American Embassy in India pointed out in a report on 'a feasible program for US economic assistance for India', that 'India is a democratic country and is the largest free country in Asia. . . . It is in competition with communist China in the sense of demonstrating the superior capacity of democracy in Asia for economic achievement for the people.'[39] The theme of India as a model was to have extensive ideological and even scientific consequences. For example, the end of the 1950s witnessed the emergence of a new endeavour in the field of political science, aiming at understanding the specificity of India's political system that was to publish its first results in the 1960s. One may quote here Rajni Kothari, arguably the first specialist to systematically try and explain why India's democracy was not altered by the existence of a '*one-dominant party*' (as the Congress party was then defined by most of the American authors) but on the contrary was strengthened by what he called the '*Congress system*' with its internal diversity.[40] This 'system', Kothari wrote, represents a '*significant model*' for many Third World countries looking for development, stability, and democracy.[41]

Diplomatically too, the notion of a 'model' had many implications. As a National Security Council report put it in 1951: 'The outcome of the competition between communist China and India as to which can best satisfy the aspirations of peoples for economic improvement will have a profound effect throughout Asia and Africa. Similarly, the relative advantages to be derived from economic co-operation with the

Soviet Bloc or the West will be closely watched.'[42] The concept would indeed have added more spice to the USA-USSR competition for India's favour. It could only annoy China which implicitly served as the non-democratic 'model', and had to accept that a significant part of the Soviet economic aid went to India.

As far as India itself was concerned, to serve as a democratic model in Asia and the world was probably gratifying. It strengthened the way India projected its image in the international sphere and particularly the symbolic aspect of its power. Relying more on the 'meaning' of its policy than on its 'power', India had always emphasized the ethical aspects of its diplomacy.[43] This was beneficial since it allowed not to spend too much for defence and to focus on economic development. Being a 'model' in terms of peaceful intention, India could hope to make use of this image to force China not to use force in order to solve the India-China border dispute. As an example of a democratic alternative to communism, was India also being conceived as a counterweight to Communist China, Washington asked?[44] The answer of President Eisenhower was clearly no, for two very pragmatic reasons: first 'India simply could not afford to play role of a counterweight' and second, 'the task would be so great [for the USA] that we would probably bankrupt ourselves in the process'.[45] The model concept did not provide a deterrent for China in 1962. On the contrary, in humiliating India, Beijing tried precisely to destroy such a concept.[46]

The 1962 India-China conflict and the 1965 India-Pakistan war posed major difficulties for the USA. Events showed that the USA was unable to overcome the contradictions of its policy toward South Asia. At the centre of the scene lay the India-Pakistan relationship. The archives reveal beyond doubt that Washington would have loved to reduce tension between the two countries and to have two friends in the subcontinent. However, achieving this goal was like trying to square the circle. Washington wanted Pakistan to remain its military ally, which meant that India was bound to look somewhere else—which was towards USSR—for support. Washington wanted to help India against China, which meant that an unhappy Pakistan would turn its eyes somewhere else—that is towards China—for additional support. The result of these contradictions was seen both in 1962 and in 1965. The main consequence was the bolstering of the USSR position in the region, at the cost ironically of its novel and deep hostility with China. The 1966 Tashkent agreement between India and Pakistan illustrated the phenomenon: the USA had to accept the Soviet influence on the subcontinent and to keep a relatively low profile in the zone. The emergence of USSR as a major power in the region (Moscow and Delhi drafted their 1971 Friendship Treaty as early as 1968-9) constituted one of the distinctive features of the period.

As seen from Washington, the Indo-Pakistan tension represented the crux of the contradiction. Kashmir remained the most nagging issue. It was on this very point that the Americans appeared the most helpless. 'Our leverage is demonstrably low', recognized Washington.[47] 'We agonise at Indo-Pakistan enmity', Secretary of State Dean Rusk told Ambassador Chester Bowles in India, adding that 'US distress at contrast between what could be achieved on subcontinent through Indo-Pakistan co-operation and what is being accomplished. This is a tragedy for India as well as US.'[48] Nothing else illustrated this 'tragedy' better than the Sandys-Harriman mission which was sent from London and Washington to India and Pakistan after the end of the hostilities with China.[49] American diplomacy came up against an insurmountable difficulty: its contradictory goals were not shared by either India or Pakistan. Fundamentally, Washington aimed at containing Communist China and at seeing India as a potential partner to achieve this. When President Kennedy met President Radhakrishnan in 1963, he expressed his desire 'to help India both economically and militarily'. But at the same time, Kennedy underlined that enhancing India's security had to be done 'without heavy cost in terms of our [America's] relations with Pakistan'. The whole problem was to fix the '*point short of causing a real crisis in Pakistan*'.[50] It is precisely this 'point' that the Sandys-Harriman mission could not achieve. Firstly, Washington had to swallow the Sino-Pakistan rapprochement initiated by Ayub Khan who wanted to offset American help to India. Ayub's move, of course, infuriated India much more than the US.[51] Secondly, Washington (and London) attempted to pressure India and Pakistan into reaching an agreement on Kashmir. In concrete geographical terms, the pressure would have entailed a larger cost for India than for Pakistan. This particularly upset Nehru.[52] To understand the Indian reaction, it is important to consider John K. Galbraith's suggestion, the then US Ambassador to India, for the fifth round of negotiations on Kashmir (Karachi, 22-25 April). He proposed to 'strike a crude bazaar level political bargain with Nehru. We would offer India defence production assistance, back up support on air, and sizeable long-term aid. We would ask in return that India promises to offer Pakistan . . . a substantial position in the guaranties on the rivers.'[53] True, Rusk rejected Galbraith's proposals but he rejected them not because they were bound to undermine India's pride, but because they were 'designed to purchase not a settlement, but an immediate breakthrough from Indian side'. And this was considered by Dean Rusk and Kennedy as going beyond what Pakistan would accept. Dean Rusk wrote: 'The price is an open-ended military commitment to India. Since this is just the thing which the Pakistanis fear most, we would expect them to react violently. This would reduce the likelihood of a Kashmir settlement and increase Indo-Pakistan tensions. We would, therefore, suffer a severe setback in our efforts to strengthen sub-continental defence against communist China. Moreover, we would risk losing the special advantages of our relationship with Pakistan.'[54] In other words, Washington had too many delicate situations to traverse at the same time: the Sandys-Harriman mission failed, but not without engendering rancour both in Pakistan and in India.

After 1971: The Importance of Being China

In 1971, the US put an end to its Chinese and South Asian headache. Kissinger's secret trip to Beijing in July and Nixon's public announcement a week later of his proposed visit to China (it would take place in February 1972) opened a new era in the Cold War. As far as South Asia was concerned, India was to bear the consequences of the Sino-US rapprochement. And even more so because the process was to take place in the midst of the Bangladesh crisis. Fundamentally, as China became America's new favoured partner, India lost much of its importance in Washington's eyes.

In deciding to establish a new partnership with China, Nixon and Kissinger decisively clarified their international strategy.[55] Communism was no longer the enemy. Indeed this notion had become inoperative in the context of the Sino-Soviet split. Soviet Union as a state became the singular geopolitical target of the United States. This did not mean, of course, that the USA would not try to establish better relations with the USSR. Bilateral and multilateral dialogues were to continue between the two main powers of the period. Meanwhile Washington had to pay attention to Chinese susceptibilities: Kissinger thus took enough care in pointing out to the Chinese the exact frame of US cooperation with the USSR. It was very important for Washington not to allow the Chinese leaders to think that the ongoing US-Soviet relations would represent a potential threat for Beijing.[56] It just meant that the US had decided to simplify its life: it was always more comfortable to have one enemy (USSR) than two (China and USSR). After 1971, for Washington China had become 'a friend' and USSR just 'a partner'.[57] China became a tacit ally of USA against the Soviet Union. The expression 'tacit alliance' is used explicitly in a background note for Kissinger's visit to Beijing in 1974.[58]

It would be beyond the scope of this paper to discuss at length the notion of a tacit alliance. However, as it is relevant to understand the global framework of Delhi-Washington-Beijing triangular relations, it seems necessary to spell it out to an extent. As far as the Cold War was concerned, as Kissinger stated in one of his memorandum to Nixon, 'the US regards the Soviet Union as our [emphasis in the original] principal national security problem and our firm policy is to work everywhere and in every way to counter Soviet expansionism and to moderate Soviet behaviour'. What did this mean in case of a war? Kissinger's answer was neat. First 'we would not [underlined in the original] welcome a Sino-Soviet war'. Secondly, 'if the Soviet Union attacks China, the United States would regard this as a threat to international stability and American security. Should the Soviet Union attack China, we are determinate to oppose it, by our decision and without any arrangement with China.'[59]

As far as politics was concerned, the array of agreements between China and USA was impressive. As President Nixon said to Chairman Mao during their first meeting: 'we can find a common ground, despite our differences, to build a world structure in which both can be safe to develop in our own ways on our own roads'.[60] This building of a 'world structure' was construed as a systematic joint effort to counter the USSR and its friends/allies everywhere in the world. 'I like rightists', Mao Zedong said to Nixon at the beginning of their first talk.[61] 'We don't like this Left', echoed Vice Premier Deng Xiaoping to Kissinger in 1974 while referring to the Communist parties of France and Italy.[62] The consequences of this vision were drawn extensively in Europe, Africa and Latin America. The memoranda of discussions between the Chinese and American leaders from 1971 to 1974 indicate that President Nixon, Kissinger, President Ford and the Chinese leaders basically agreed in their strategic approaches vis-à-vis Portugal (concerning the Communist push during the 1974 Revolution), Spain (concerning the necessity to organize a smooth transition from Franco to the monarchy), France (concerning the necessity to contain the French Communist Party's weight), Yugoslavia (concerning the post-

Tito era), Europe at large (concerning the strengthening of its unity and of NATO), Chile (concerning the necessity to check the pro-Soviet Communist forces) and in Greece, Turkey, Zaire, Angola, etc.[63]

The Chinese leadership's determination to implement their strategy is striking when surveying the archives. It constituted the basis of their new relationship with the USA. For instance, when a difficulty arose in a bilateral conversation, Kissinger always took care to remind the Chinese—usually through a joke—that the Russians were their real enemy. The Chinese would then gleefully nod their assent.[64] To summarize: the Sino-US rapprochement suddenly opened a new space for American diplomacy in the region. India was the first country to feel its effect. Kissinger wrote to Nixon in August 1974:

> The Chinese see the 'southern rim' of Asia—the area stretching from Turkey, Iran, Afghanistan to India, Pakistan, and Bangladesh to Southeast Asia—as an integrated whole. They see the Soviet Union seeking to penetrate this area in an effort to encircle China. The Chinese leaders have asked us to pay attention to this area, to support our friends there, and to help block Soviet penetration. We have stated that we agree with this analysis.[65]

The first consequence for New Delhi, as far as the Americans were concerned, was that India was no longer perceived as a country that had to be supported and if necessary defended against Communist China. Thus, part of its relevance for the Western bloc had disappeared. This was, of course, a very significant change. The whole American strategy up to 1971 was based on the premise that India had to be 'instrumentalized' against the strong USSR-China alliance. Ironically, Washington based henceforth its policy on what India had been telling America since 1947, that is the existence of a strong Sino-Soviet divergence. In 1964, Dean Rusk was still sure that such a divergence could not be of any use to the USA. On the contrary, Indian Defence Minister, Y.B. Chavan, at a meeting in Washington commented on the lasting character of the Sino-Soviet rift. Rusk answered that 'we [the USA] have, nevertheless, assumed neither Soviets nor Chicoms could afford [to] see other punished in conflict with capitalist nations. Therefore, we assumed alliance would not be dissolved. . . . Sino-Soviet split [is] important but not complete enough for either US or India to rely on.'[66]

The change in the American vision allowed American diplomacy to cut its Gordian knot in South Asia. In particular, Washington no longer felt the necessity to maintain the equilibrium between India and

Pakistan. The tilt went definitively in favour of Pakistan. And more so because Washington and Beijing had established their new relationships thanks to Pakistan's help. The 1971 Kissinger's secret visit to Beijing started from Islamabad. During a meeting with Kissinger, the Pakistani Ambassador to the USA, Agha Hilaly, reminded him of the Secretary of State William Rogers visit to Pakistan in 1969 in which the latter had mentioned about Nixon's interest in improving relations with China. He then recalled that Nixon himself during his visit in Lahore (August 1969) had mentioned this to President Yahya Khan. Acknowledging Pakistan's support in bridging the gap between Washington and Beijing, Kissinger replied that 'our gratitude is very great'.[67]

India also became the subcontinent's 'bad guy' in the eyes of Washington. Everything happened as if Nixon and Kissinger were telling the Chinese that 'the friend of your enemy cannot be our friend'. India was now seen by Washington as a pawn in the Soviet strategy towards South Asia. Saying he failed to understand the policy of India, Kissinger told the Indian Ambassador in Washington, L.K. Jha, in August 1971 that everything was happening as if India wanted to become 'an extension of Soviet foreign policy'.[68] The anti-Indian thrust of the US policy was, one may say, the natural consequence of its new compulsions. However, the American tirade vis-à-vis India that is found in the archives needs probably some further explanations. I will point out three factors.

The first one concerns the global balance of power towards the beginning of the 1970s. One just need to recall that the America was facing hard times, especially with the disastrous military campaign in Vietnam. The USSR's influence was at its zenith and Washington perceived Moscow's growing influence in South Asia as a direct threat to its own position in the Indian Ocean. India's position on this constituted a major source of irritation. To some extent, Delhi's policy was an enigma for Kissinger and Nixon. Both of them were addicted to 'realpolitik'. Kissinger took obvious pleasure in occasionally quoting Metternich during his talks with the Chinese leaders who liked to flatter him in recalling his talents as a historian and a philosopher. How could a 'potentially' great power like India allow its policy to be dictated by Soviet Union? Kissinger asked the Indian Ambassador to the US, L.K. Jha. Jha's answer was certainly not the most appropriate to convince Kissinger that India was not pro-soviet.[69] He chose to say that 'first of all, Madame Gandhi was not at all pro-Soviet'. Then, Jha suggested that the 1971 Indo-Soviet treaty 'had first been thought up long time ago by Dinesh Singh, the former Foreign Minister', adding 'on a personal basis [that] he wouldn't be a bit surprised if Dinesh Singh actually received pay from the Communists.' Jha adds that '[T.N.] Kaul and [P.N.] Haksar were very much under Soviet influence' and that 'for both these reasons Madame Gandhi was under great pressure'. In fact, 'she did not have her heart in it [the treaty]'. He ended his meeting with Kissinger in repeating that 'Haksar and Kaul were the real obstacles in India and that in the Foreign Office there were many pro-Soviet elements'.

The second factor concerns the immediate reason for the Indo-American estrangement. The Sino-US rapprochement took place in the midst of the Bangladesh crisis. Nixon and Kissinger did not want to convey to Beijing the impression that the USA, as China's new friend, was so weak that it could not solve a regional crisis where their ally Pakistan was involved. Washington, thus, had no other choice but to show its muscle. True, Nixon and Kissinger had expected that the Soviet Union—thanks to the 1971 treaty—would try to put some pressure on Delhi and would moderate India's policy toward Pakistan. But as events progressed, Kissinger estimated that India not only wanted to favour Bangladesh's independence, but to attack West Pakistan as well. Without any concrete proof—except for a CIA report—and refusing to listen to clear Indian denials, Kissinger based his policy on a wrong assumption. He was to go to the extent of trying to indirectly encourage China to help Pakistan militarily. It was in this context that Nixon and Kissinger decided to send the aircraft carrier *Enterprise* to the Bay of Bengal in December 1971. On this point, the archives fully confirm Dennis Kux's appreciation on the event.[70] Kissinger was wrong twice in speculating that the conflict would spread: he misread India's intention which was never to attack West Pakistan, and he misread China's policy which never intended to enter in a war against India for Pakistan. The Chinese in fact never wanted the Bangladesh crisis to go beyond a certain limit, one reason being that they did not want to run the risk of a military confrontation with the USSR.

The third factor concerns the depth of Kissinger and Nixon's anti-India feelings. India was perceived, notably by Nixon who always retained memories of an unpleasant first visit of India as Vice President in 1953. Nixon and Kissinger expectedly had also no personal esteem for the Soviet leadership and diplomats. They conveyed this feeling to the Chinese when they discussed the Russians. As the Chinese leaders shared the same perception in a more crude way, the tone of the American-Chinese conversations was often plainly anti-Indian.[71] 'I have never been an admirer of Indian policy', Kissinger told Zhou Enlai, adding that he 'suddenly realised they [the Indians] had been bringing pressure on you' during the Sino-Indian war, after having visited India in 1962 and after having talked to Krishna Menon. The Chinese contempt for India could be clearly perceived during the same conversation. Zhou Enlai joked about Nehru who told him that he was from Kashmir, which therefore proved that Kashmir was Indian territory. 'India', he added, 'cannot be considered as a small country but still stoops to such tricks. A small country could perhaps win at doing such things, though perhaps some small nations would have more backbone than that.'[72] On his part, Kissinger, as he was talked of Hegel, depicted Indian philosophy as a 'very passive philosophy', which 'never meant to have a practical application'. 'It's just a bunch of empty words', answered Mao. Kissinger pointed out that Gandhi's non-violence 'wasn't a philosophic principle', but 'essentially a tactical device for him'. It was 'a revolutionary tactic, not an ethical principle'; 'because he [Gandhi] thought the British were too moralistic and sentimental to use violence'.[73] By contrast, Kissinger saw the Western intellectual being a romantic entertaining erroneous ideas about India. 'India', he said to Zhou Enlai, 'has a considerable influence on our domestic public opinion, not so much on the public at large which does not like it, but on the intellectuals which have had a romantic idea about India as a non violent country'.[74] He himself did not share the 'English romantic tradition toward India'.[75] This explained in his view the position of some British leaders during the Bangladesh war. Kissinger regretted that in his own country, 'there is a sentimental love affair between Western intellectuals and India based on a complete misreading of the Indian philosophy of life'.[76]

The Containment of India

After 1971, it was no longer US policy to contain China. By contrast, India had to be contained, at least to some extent. On the one hand, India represented an important regional power that might be of some value and use to Washington. It was not a Communist State and for this reason could not be put on par with China. 'Our interest in the long term [are] congruent', Kissinger told L.K. Jha in August 1971.[77]

In 1972, he promised the Indian Ambassador that 'if China is engaged in military adventures against India, we would not support it at all'.[78] In 1973, he told Jha again that 'we will continue our relations with the Chinese, but we do not pursue Chinese objectives in the sub-continent'. 'With respect to Bangladesh', Kissinger pointed out, 'our interest are like yours, that is, in the stability of the country. We do not want a Communist Bangladesh, nor do you . . . it would have a catastrophic effect on West Bengal.'[79] Two years after the Bangladesh war, American perspectives had changed somewhat.

Being then ready to recognize India's regional role—so long as this phenomenon did not hurt US national interest—Washington noticeably paid a lot of attention to the strengthened Soviet position in the region. In this respect, at the beginning of the 1970s, China was a much more valuable friend than India while Pakistan represented an important asset. The 1973 Baluchistan uprising and the 1974 Daud's anti-monarchy coup in Afghanistan illustrated the importance of US-Chinese connections in this part of the world. Washington was afraid of a building Moscow–Kabul–New Delhi axis that could weaken Pakistan. America sought to counterbalance the axis by relying on Iran and China. This would inevitably involve military help to Pakistan and the Shah of Iran, a development that could only raise India's anxiety levels.[80]

As far as China was concerned, it fully cooperated with the US to help both Pakistan and Iran in suppressing the Baluchistani revolt (one estimate reckons that 9,000 people died in Baluchistan). During this period, Zhou Enlai repeatedly insisted that the US should send weapons to Pakistan.[81] Kissinger underlined that it was not easy to do so, because of the public opinion in the US and the opposition inside the Congress. The Chinese then proposed that the US government should act through Iran. Kissinger answered that was precisely the reason why he decided to send former CIA Director Richard Helms to Iran, as the coordinator of the US policy in the region. Washington and Beijing felt that the Afghan political developments and the Baluchistan question were inter-related. Prince Daud is 'well known as having some pro-Soviet orientation', Kissinger said. 'The final intention of Soviet Union is to get it all in the Soviet hand', added Zhou Enlai.[82] When President Ford met Deng Xiaoping in Beijing in 1973, they both agreed that the Soviet Union 'has not given up its plan for Baluchistan' (Deng) and that 'the major thing is to keep the Indians out of Pakistan' (Kissinger).[83] The Chinese then went on to tell Kissinger that 'it is better to have you in India than the Soviet alone'[84] and to suggest to Washington to assist Islamabad in 'building a naval port' in Pakistan.[85] Kissinger and his main aide, Winston Lord (Director, Policy Planning Staff, Department of State), went to the extent of suggesting although jokingly that Washington should give nuclear weapons to Pakistan to contain hegemonistic India.[86] The contrast with the views prevailing before 1971 was complete.

Notes

1. *Foreign Relations of the United States* (hereafter *FRUS*), *1947*, vol. 3, p. 171.
2. *FRUS, 1947*, vol. 3, p. 151.
3. Ibid., p. 179.
4. Ibid., p. 138.
5. Ibid., p. 147.
6. *FRUS, 1948*, vol. 5, p. 506.
7. Ibid., p. 242.
8. *FRUS, 1950*, vol. 5, p. 246.
9. *FRUS, 1949*, vol. 6, p. 1756.
10. *FRUS, 1948*, vol. 5, p. 504.
11. *FRUS, 1950*, vol. 5, p. 1475.
12. *FRUS, 1948*, vol. 5, p. 278.
13. *FRUS, 1950*, vol. 5, p. 182.
14. Ibid., p. 200.
15. Memorandum, Near Eastern, South Asian and African Affairs to Senators of State. Ibid., p. 169.
16. Ibid.
17. Study, National Security Council, *FRUS, 1952-54*, vol. 11, p. 1997. This is also the opinion of the CIA. CIA Memorandum, *FRUS, 1950*, vol. 5, p. 1493.
18. Department of State Policy Statement. Ibid.
19. Said the Director of the Near Eastern, South Asian and African Affairs. Ibid., p. 184.
20. Ibid., p. 246.
21. Nehru's visit to South-East Asia was highly appreciated by Washington. Nehru 'talked to his audiences . . . as few foreigners would have dared' and 'in speaking so frankly Nehru served our interest admirably'. Memorandum, Near Eastern, South Asian and African Affairs to the Secretary of State, Ibid., p. 1467.
22. For example, in 1950, the American Ambassador in India was aware of the Patel/Nehru divergences on foreign policy ('[Patel] was convinced . . . that continuation of Nehru's policy would endanger security of India . . . he felt so strangely in the matter that he would prefer to resign from Cabinet and to break openly with Nehru rather than to allow matters to drift').

The Ambassador added: 'it might be embarrassing if change of GOI policy would be based on expectation of receiving substantial military equipment from US in view of our own shortages in this respect'. Ibid., p. 1475.

23. Conversation with the American Ambassador in India, *FRUS, 1951*, vol. 6, p. 2184.
24. Ibid., p. 2188.
25. Ibid., p. 2184.
26. Ibid., p. 2188.
27. Ibid., p. 2189
28. Ibid., p. 2184.
29. Ibid., p. 2125.
30. *FRUS, 1948*, vol. 5, p. 520.
31. Ibid.
32. *FRUS, 1949*, vol. 6, p. 1755.
33. *FRUS, 1951*, vol. 6, p. 2184.
34. *FRUS, 1949*, vol. 6, p. 1752.
35. *FRUS, 1951*, vol. 6, p. 2188.
36. Ibid., p. 2176.
37. 'US policy towards the South Asia region', Ibid., p. 4.
38. See Gilles Boquérat, *No Strings Attached? India's Policies and Foreign Aid, 1947-1966*, Delhi: Manohar, 2003.
39. *FRUS, 1955-1957*, vol. 8, p. 312.
40. Rajni Kothari, 'The Congress System in India', *Asian Survey*, 4 (12), December 1964, pp. 1161-73.
41. Rajni Kothari, *Politics in India*, New Delhi: Orient Longman, 1970, pp. 8-9.
42. Statement of policy on US policy towards South Asia, 10 January 1951, *FRUS, 1955-1957*, vol. 3, p. 31.
43. We use here the terms 'meaning' and 'power' according to Zaki Laidi's definitions. Zaki Laidi, *Power and Purpose after the Cold War*, Oxford: Berg Publishers, 1994.
44. Paper prepared by the National Security Council Planning Board, 26 May 1959, *FRUS, 1958-1960*, vol. 15, p. 4.
45. Memorandum of discussion at the 408th meeting of the National Security Council, 28 May 1959. Ibid., p. 9.
46. In 1963, President Radhakrishnan told President Kennedy that China's intention was 'to show that India was not strong enough to stand against China' and to 'disrupt the Indian democratic way of life', so that 'other countries would give up their struggles for democracy and go China's way'. *FRUS, 1961-1963*, vol. 19, p. 609.
47. Memorandum from the Executive Secretary of the Department of State to the President's Special Assistant for National Security Affairs, 27 January 1964, *FRUS, 1964-1968*, vol. 25, p. 22.

48. Telegram, 22 May 1964. Ibid., pp. 105-6.
49. W. Averell Harriman was then Under Secretary of State for Political Affairs and Duncan Sandys was the Commonwealth Relations Secretary. For a detailed account of the mission, see Dennis Kux, *The United States and Pakistan, 1947-2000. Disenchanted Allies*. Baltimore: The Johns Hopkins University Press, 2001, pp. 134-44.
50. Memorandum of conversation, 3 June 1964. *FRUS, 1961-1963*, vol. 19, p. 610.
51. Pakistan signed a border agreement with China (concerning the part of Kashmir under Pakistan control) and opened a civil aviation link with China. This last decision led Washington to impose economic sanctions for the first time against Karachi.
52. See telegram from the Embassy in India to the Department of State, 15 April 1963, *FRUS, 1961-1963*, vol. 19, p. 276. Galbraith told Nehru that a settlement 'could only be accomplished by dividing the Valley with appropriate arrangements'. Nehru then 'once or twice . . . got very angry, shouted and pounded the table.'
53. Ibid., p. 530.
54. Ibid.
55. As we know, these two American leaders played an important personal role. A large part of the American diplomacy did not agree with Kissinger's vision and method. In fact, the State Department was kept away from Nixon's initiative on China.
56. See for example the care with which Kissinger informed the Chinese Ambassador in Washington (Huang) and the Deputy Chief of the People's Republic of China Liaison Office (Han Hou) in 1973 about his discussions with Brezhnev. *Nixon Papers*, National Security Council, Memorandum of conversations, 6 July 1973 and 15 May 1973.
57. Kissinger reported to the Chinese representative in Washington his discussions with the Soviet leader Brezhnev: 'he [Brezhnev] said, "do you consider China an ally?". I said, "no, we don't consider it an ally—we consider it a friend." He said, "well you can have any friends you want, but you and me should be partners"—he meant Moscow and Washington', Memorandum of conversation, 15 May 1973.
58. 'The Sino-Soviet-US triangle. We have been in probably the ideal situation with regard to the two communist giants; they both want and need to deal with us because they cannot deal with one another. We are walking a delicate tightrope of détente with Moscow and a tacit alliance with Peking.' Policy Planning Council, Director's Files (Winston Lord), *RG* 59, box 374 (folder: China Sensitive. Special Winston Lord file. Misc. and reports, November 1974), August 1974, p. 8.
59. Memorandum for the President from H.A. Kissinger, Commitments to the PRC, Draft, August 1974, Policy Planning Council, Director's Files (Winston

Lord), *RG* 59, box 371 (folder: Secretary's visit to Peking. Bilateral issues. s/p Mr Lord. November 1974).

60. Memorandum of conversation, 21 February 1972, Policy Planning Council, Director's Files (Winston Lord), *RG* 59, box 372 (folder: Mao Book, December 1975, Mr Lord).
61. Ibid.
62. Policy Planning Council, Director's files, memorandum of conversations, 27 November 1974, *RG* 59, box 372 (folder: Secretary Kissinger's talk in China, 25-29 November 1974).
63. An extract from a conversation between President Ford and Mao: *President Ford* 'And we support the new King [of Spain] because the whole belly of Western Europe must remain strong—Portugal, Spain, Italy, Greece, Turkey, Yugoslavia. All that must be strengthened if we are to meet any expansionist efforts by the Soviet Union'. *Chairman Mao*: 'Good. Yes, and we think Greece should get better'. *President Ford* : 'Yes. . . . And we hope they will come back as full partner in NATO.' *Chairman Mao* : 'That would be good', memorandum of conversation, 2 December 1975, Policy Planning Council, Director's Files (Winston Lord), *RG* 59, box 373 (folder: Mao/Ford, Hak–4:10–6 pm).
64. For example, in 1975, Deng Xiaoping compared Brezhnev's policy to Hitler's policy and pressed the USA not to follow a Munich policy of appeasement vis-à-vis Moscow. See memorandum of conversation between Deng Xiaoping and Ford, 1 December 1975, Policy Planning Council, Director's Files (Winston Lord), *RG* 59, box 373.
65. Memorandum for the President from Kissinger, August 1974, already quoted.
66. Telegram from the Department of State to the Embassy in India, 22 May 1964. *FRUS, 1964-1968*, vol. 25, p. 105.
67. Memorandum of conversation, 21 July 1971, *Nixon Papers*, National Security Council, box 643 (folder: India/Pakistan).
68. Memorandum of conversation, 25 August 1971, *Nixon Papers*, National Security Council, box 643 (folder: India/Pakistan).
69. Memorandum of conversation, 9 August 1971, *Nixon Papers*, National Security Council, box 643 (folder: India/Pakistan).
70. Dennis Kux, *The United States and Pakistan*, pp. 200-3.
71. In one of his conversations with Kissinger, Mao tells the Soviet leaders are 'bastards'. Memorandum of conversation, 17 February 1973, Policy Planning Council, Director's files (Winston Lord), *RG* 59, box 372 (folder: Mao Book, Dec. 75- E).
72. Memorandum of conversation, 18 February 1973, *Nixon Papers*, National Security Council, box 98 (folder: HAK China trip, February 1973, Chicoms reports (originals).
73. Memorandum of conversation between Kissinger and Mao Zedong, 12 November 1973, Policy Planning Council, Director's files (Winston Lord), *RG* 59, box 372 (folder: Mao Book, December 1975, Mr Lord).

74. Memorandum of conversation between Kissinger and Zhou Enlai, 11 November 1973, *Nixon Papers*, National Security Council, box 95 (folder: Secretary Kissinger conversation in Peking, November 1973).
75. Memorandum of conversation between Kissinger and Zhou Enlai, 16 February 1973, *Nixon Papers*, National Security Council, box 95 (folder: China President's talks with Mao and Zhou Enlai, February 1972).
76. Memorandum of conversation between Mao and Kissinger, 12 November 1973, National Security Council, *RG* 59, box 372 (Mao Book, Dec. 1975, Mr. Lord).
77. Memorandum of conversation, 30 August 1971, *Nixon Papers*, National Security Council, Box 643 (folder: India/Pakistan, July 1971-Nov. 30, 1971).
78. Memorandum of conversation, 22 September 1972, Ibid., box 130 (folder: memcom's, May 1971- Sept. 1973, HAK/Amb. Jha and Amb. Kaul of India).
79. Memorandum of conversation, 29 January 1973, Ibid.
80. For example, T.N. Kaul (the then Indian Ambassador in Washington) denied any Indian interest in Baluchistan's uprising when Kissinger asked him about it (see *Nixon Papers*, memorandum of conversation, 15 August 1973, box 1030). However, he did not agree with military aid (Phantom) given by Washington to Iran. 'Iran wants to dominate the Gulf', he said to Kissinger (memorandum of conversation, 14 July 1974, Ibid.).
81. Memorandum of conversation between Kissinger and Zhou Enlai, 18 February 1973, *Nixon Papers*, National Security Council, Box 95 (folder: HAK China trip, Feb. 1973, memcoms). Reports (originals).
82. Memorandum of conversation between Kissinger and Zhou Enlai, 11 November 1973. Ibid. (folder: Secretary Kissinger's conversation in Peking, November 1972).
83. Memorandum of conversation between Deng Xiaoping and Ford, 3 December 1975, Policy Planning Council, Director's files (Winston Lord), *RG* 59, box 373 (folder: President Ford's trip to China, 1-5 December 1975).
84. Memorandum of conversation, 27 November 1974, Ibid., box 372 (folder: Secretary Kissinger's talk in China, 25-29 November 1974).
85. Memorandum of conversation between Zhou Enlai and Kissinger, 14 November 1973, *Nixon Papers*, National Security Council, box 92 (folder: Secretary Kissinger's conversations in Peking, November 1973).
86. See the conversation between Kissinger and Deng Xiaoping, 27 November 1974: '*Vice Premier Deng*: "Recently you visited India, and after your visit you improved your relations with India, and we believe that this was a good move. Because if there is only the Soviet Union [there they will be the only ones with influence], it is better to have you in India that the Soviets alone." *Secretary Kissinger*: "That was the intention of the trip. And it also will make it easier to do things in Pakistan without being accused of an anti-Indian motivation. [Deng spits loudly into his spittoon beside his chair]. And as you know, we have invited Prime Minister Bhutto to Washington, and after that,

there will be some concrete progress." *Vice Premier Deng*: "I think you said it would be possible for you to sell weapons to Pakistan. But will Pakistan be able to pay?" *Secretary Kissinger*: "Yes." *Vice Premier Deng*: "That would be good. As for India, you mentioned earlier that India was hegemonistic.' *Secretary Kissinger*: "It is my assessment. One of my colleagues said he was not only in favour of giving arms to Pakistan, but arms and nuclear weapons to Pakistan and Bangladesh." [Ambassador Huang laughingly leans across the table and wags his pencil at Mr. Lord]. Mr. Lord [Laughter], head of our Policy Planning Staff.' Policy Planning Council. Director's files (Winston Lord 1969-77, General Records of the Department of State, *RG* 59, box 372 (folder Secretary Kissinger's talk in China, 25-29 November 1974), 27 November 1974: 13.

❖ Contributors

GILLES BOQUÉRAT, a specialist of South Asian affairs, is currently the head of the Department of International Relations at the CSH (Centre de Sciences Humaines) in New Delhi. He is also a member of the CEIAS (Centre d'Etudes de l'Inde et de l'Asie du Sud, Paris). He has authored a number of articles on international and regional politics in South Asia and has recently published a book on foreign aid and politics in India during the Cold War (*No Strings Attached?*, New Delhi: Manohar, 2003) for which he has extensively used American, British and French archival documents.

DENNIS KUX, is a former ambassador and a retired State Department South Asia specialist. He is currently a senior scholar at the Woodrow Wilson International Center for Scholars and has authored two seminal works on American relations with India and Pakistan for which archival materials have been extensively used: *Estranged Democracies, India and the United States 1941-1991* (Washington: National Defence University Press, 1993) and *The United States and Pakistan 1947-2000, Disenchanted Allies* (Baltimore: The John Hopkins University Press, 2001)

SERGEY LOUNEV is a leading research fellow of Institute of World Economy and International Relations, Russian Academy of Sciences, and teaches at the Moscow State University. He is the author of many monographs: *Diplomacy in South Asia* (Moscow: Science-Oriental Literature, 1993); *Russia, China and India in the Modern Global Processes* (Moscow: Moscow Public Science Foundation, 1998); *The Challenges to the Security of the Southern Boundaries of Russia* (Moscow: Moscow Public Science Foundation, 1999); *Independent Republics of Central Asia and Russia* (Moscow: Institute of Oriental Studies, 2001) and *Transformation of the World System: The Role of Largest States of Eurasia* (Moscow: Academia, 2001).

MAX-JEAN ZINS is a senior researcher of the CNRS (Centre National de la Recherche Scientifique). He is presently attached to the CERI

(Centre d'Etudes et de Recherches Internationales, Paris) and is an associate member of the CEIAS (Centre d'Etudes de l'Inde et de l'Asie du Sud, Paris). His latest book (in French) is titled *Pakistan: The Quest for Identity* (Paris: Belin-La Documentation Française, 2001). For the project concerning this book, he has been associated with the Woodrow Wilson Center in Washington for one month in November 2001.